Mary Hartwell Catherwood

Heroes of the Middle West

The French

Mary Hartwell Catherwood

Heroes of the Middle West
The French

ISBN/EAN: 9783337190194

Printed in Europe, USA, Canada, Australia, Japan

Cover: Foto ©ninafisch / pixelio.de

More available books at **www.hansebooks.com**

HEROES OF THE MIDDLE WEST

COUNT FRONTENAC.

From a Statue at Quebec.

HEROES OF THE
MIDDLE WEST

The French

BY

MARY HARTWELL CATHERWOOD

BOSTON, U.S.A.

GINN AND COMPANY

The Athenæum Press

1898

PREFACE.

LET any one who thinks it an easy task attempt to cover the French discovery and occupation of the middle west, from Marquette and Jolliet to the pulling down of the French flag on Fort Chartres, vivifying men, and while condensing events, putting a moving picture before the eye. Let him prepare this picture for young minds accustomed only to the modern aspect of things and demanding a light, sure touch. Let him gather his material — as I have done — from Parkman, Shea, Joutel, Hennepin, St. Cosme, Monette, Winsor, Roosevelt — from state records, and local traditions richer and oftener more reliable than history; and let him hang over his theme with brooding affection, moulding and remoulding its forms. He will find the task he so lightly set himself a terribly hard and exhausting one, and will appreciate as he never before appreciated the labors of those who work in historic fields.

v

CONTENTS.

HEROES OF THE MIDDLE WEST.

I.

THE DISCOVERERS OF THE UPPER MISSISSIPPI.

THE 17th of May, 1673, Father Jacques
Marquette, the missionary priest of St. Ignace,
on what is now called the north shore of Michigan, and Louis Jolliet, a trader from Montreal,
set out on a journey together.

Huron and Ottawa Indians, with the priest
left in charge of them, stood on the beach to
see Marquette embark, — the water running up
to their feet and receding with the everlasting
wash of the straits. Behind them the shore
line of St. Ignace was bent like a long bow.
Northward, beyond the end of the bow, a rock
rose in the air as tall as a castle. But very
humble was the small mission station which
Father Marquette had founded when driven
with his flock from his post on the Upper
Lakes by the Iroquois. A chapel of strong

1

cedar posts covered with bark, his own hut,
and the lodges of his people were all surrounded
by pointed palisades.   Opposite St. Ignace,
across a league or so of water, rose the turtle-
shaped back of Michilimackinac Island, venerated by the tribes, in spite of their religious
teaching, as a home of mysterious giant fairies
who made gurgling noises in the rocks along
the beach or floated vast and cloud-like through
high pine forests.   The evergreens on Michilimackinac showed as if newborn through the
haze of undefined deciduous trees, for it was
May weather, which means that the northern
world had not yet leaped into sudden and glori-
ous summer.   Though the straits glittered under
a cloudless sky, a chill lingered in the wind,
and only the basking stone ledges reflected
warmth.   The clear elastic air was such a per-
fect medium of sight that it allowed the eye to
distinguish open beach rims from massed forests two or three leagues away on the south
shore, and seemed to bring within stone's throw
those nearer islands now called Round and Bois
Blanc.

It must have wrung Marquette's heart to leave
this region, which has an irresistible charm for
all who come within its horizon.   But he had

long desired to undertake this journey for a double purpose. He wanted to carry his religion as far as possible among strange tribes, and he wanted to find and explore that great river of the west, about which adventurers in the New World heard so much, but which none had seen.

A century earlier, its channel southward had really been taken possession of by the Spaniards, its first discoverers. But they made no use of their discovery, and on their maps traced it as an insignificant stream. The French did not know whether this river flowed into the Gulf of California — which was called the Red Sea — or to the western ocean, or through Virginia eastward. Illinois Indians, visiting Marquette's mission after the manner of roving tribes, described the father of waters and its tributaries. Count Frontenac, the governor of Canada, thought the matter of sufficient importance to send Louis Jolliet with an outfit to join the missionary in searching for the stream.

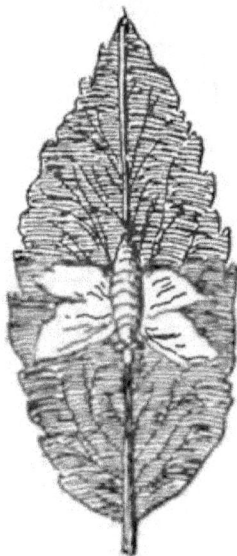

Totem of the Illinois.

The explorers took with them a party of five men. Their canoes, we are told, were of birch bark and cedar splints, the ribs being shaped from spruce roots. Covered with the pitch of yellow pine, and light enough to be carried on the shoulders of four men across portages, these canoes yet had toughness equal to any river voyage. They were provisioned with smoked meat and Indian corn. Shoved clear of the beach, they shot out on the blue water to the dip of paddles. Marquette waved his adieu. His Indians, remembering the dangers of that southern country, scarcely hoped to see him again. Marquette, though a young man, was of no such sturdy build as Jolliet. Among descendants of the Ottawas you may still hear the tradition that he had a "white face, and long hair the color of the sun" flowing to the shoulders of his black robe.

The watching figures dwindled, as did the palisaded settlement. Hugging the shore, the canoes entered Lake Michigan, or, as it was then called, the Lake of the Illinois. All the islands behind seemed to meet and intermingle and to cover themselves with blue haze as they went down on the water. Priest and trader, their skins moist with the breath of the lake, each in his own canoe, faced silently the unknown world toward which they were venturing. The shaggy coast line bristled with evergreens, and though rocky, it was low, unlike the white cliffs of Michilimackinac.

Marquette had made a map from the descriptions of the Illinois Indians. The canoes were moving westward on the course indicated by his map. He was peculiarly gifted as a missionary, for already he spoke six Indian languages, and readily adapted himself to any dialect. Marquette, the records tell us, came of "an old and honorable family of Laon," in northern France. Century after century the Marquettes bore high honors in Laon, and their armorial bearings commemorated devotion to the king in distress. In our own Revolutionary War it is said that three Marquettes fought for us with La Fayette. No young man of his time had a pleasanter or easier life offered him at home than Jacques Marquette. But he chose to devote himself to missionary labor in the New World, and had already helped to found three missions, enduring much hardship. Indian half-breeds, at what is now called the "Soo," on St. Mary's River, betwixt Lake Huron and Lake Superior, have a tradition that Father Marquette and Father Dablon built their missionary station on a tiny island of rocks, not more than two canoe lengths from shore, on the American side. But men who have written books declare it was on the bank below the rapids.

Jolliet had come of different though not less worthy stock. He was Canadian born, the son of a wagon-maker in Quebec ; and he had been

Autograph of Jolliet.

well educated, and possessed an active, adventurous mind. He was dressed for this expedition in the tough buckskin hunting suit which frontiersmen then wore. But Marquette retained the long black cassock of the priest. Their five voyageurs — or trained woodsmen — in more or less stained buckskin and caps of fur, sent the canoes shooting over the water with scarcely a sound, dipping a paddle now on this side and now on that, Indian fashion ; Marquette and Jolliet taking turns with them as the day progressed. For any man, whether voyageur, priest, or seignior, who did not know how to paddle a canoe, if occasion demanded, was at sore disadvantage in the New World.

The first day of any journey, before one meets weariness or anxiety and disappointment, remains always the freshest in memory. When the sun went down, leaving violet shadows on the chill lake, they drew their boats on shore; and Pierre Porteret and another Frenchman, named Jacques, gathered driftwood to make a fire, while the rest of the crew unpacked the cargo. They turned each canoe on its side, propping the ends with sticks driven into the ground, thus making canopies like half-roofs to shelter them for the night.

"The Sieur Jolliet says it is not always that we may light a camp-fire," said Pierre Porteret to Jacques, as he struck a spark into his tinder with the flint and steel which a woodsman carried everywhere.

"He is not likely to have one to-night, even in this safe cove," responded Jacques, kneeling to help, and anxious for supper. "Look now at me; I know the Indian way to start a blaze by taking two pieces of wood and boring one into the other, rubbing it thus between my palms.

It is a gift. Not many voyageurs can accomplish that."

"Rub thy two stupid heads together and make a blaze," said another hungry man, coming with a kettle of lake water. But the fire soon climbed pinkly through surrounding darkness. They drove down two forked supports to hold a crosspiece, and hung the kettle to boil their hulled corn. Then the fish which had been taken by trolling during the day were dressed and broiled on hot coals.

The May starlight was very keen over their heads in a dark blue sky which seemed to rise to infinite heights, for the cold northern night air swept it of every film. Their first delicious meal was blessed and eaten ; and stretched in blankets, with their feet to the camp fire, the tired explorers rested. They were still on the north shore of what we now call the state of Michigan, and their course had been due westward by the compass. A cloud of Indian tobacco smoke rose from the lowly roof of each canoe, and its odor mingled with the sweet acrid breath of burning wood. Jolliet and the voyageurs had learned to use this dried brown weed, which all tribes held in great esteem and carried about with them in their rovings.

"If true tales be told of the water around the Bay of the Puans," one of the voyageurs was heard to say as he stretched himself under the canoe allotted to the men, "we may save our salt when we pass that country."

"Have you ever heard, Father," Jolliet inquired of the missionary, "that the word Puan meant foul or ill-smelling instead of salty?"

"I know," Marquette answered, "that salt has a vile odor to the Indians. They do not use it with their food, preferring to season that instead with the sugar they make from the maple tree. Therefore, the bay into which we are soon to venture they call the Bay of the Fetid, or ill-smelling salty country, on account of saline water thereabout."

"Then why do the Winnebago tribe on this bay allow themselves to be called Puans?"

"That has never been explained by the missionaries sent to that post, though the name seems to carry no reproach. They are well made and tall of stature. I find Wild Oats a stranger name — the Menomonies are Wild Oats Indians. Since the gospel has been preached to all these tribes for some years past, I trust we may find good Christians among them."

" What else have you learned about the country ? "

" Father Dablon told me that the way to the head of that river called Fox, up which we must paddle, is as hard as the way to heaven, specially the rapids. But when you arrive there it is a natural paradise."

" We have tremendous labor before us," mused Jolliet. "Father, did you ever have speech with that Jean Nicollet, who, first of any Frenchman, got intimations of the great river ? "

" I never saw him."

" There was a man I would have traveled far to see, though he was long a renegade among savages, and returned to the settlements only to die."

" Heaven save this expedition from becoming renegade among savages by forgetting its highest object ! " breathed Marquette.

His companion smiled toward the pleasant fire-light. Jolliet had once thought of becoming a priest himself. He venerated this young apostle, only half a dozen years his senior. But he was glad to be a free adventurer, seeking wealth and honor ; not foreseeing that though the great island of Anticosti in the Gulf of St. Lawrence would be given him for his services, he would die a poor and neglected man.

When, after days of steady progress, the expedition entered the Bay of Puans, now called Green Bay, and found the nation of Menomonies or Wild Oats Indians, Marquette was as much interested as Jolliet in the grain which gave these people their bread. It grew like rice, in marshy places, on knotted stalks which appeared above the water in June and rose several feet higher. The grain seed was long and slender and made plentiful meal. The Indians gathered this volunteer harvest in September, when the kernels were so ripe that they dropped readily into canoes pushed among the stalks. They were then spread out on lattice work and smoked to dry the chaff, which could be trodden loose when the whole bulk, tied in a skin bag, was put into a hollow in the ground made for that purpose. The Indians pounded their grain to meal and cooked it with fat.

The Menomonies tried to prevent Marquette and Jolliet from going farther. They said the great river was dangerous, full of frightful monsters that swallowed both men and canoes ; that there was a roaring demon in it who could be heard for leagues ; and the heat was so intense in those southern countries through which it flowed, that if the Frenchmen escaped all other dangers, they must die of that. Marquette told them his own life was nothing compared to the good word he wanted to carry to those southern tribes, and he laughed at the demon and instructed them in his own religion.

The aboriginal tribes, by common instinct, tried from the first to keep the white man out of countries which he was determined to overrun and possess, regardless of danger.

At the end of a voyage of thirty leagues, or about ninety miles, the explorers reached the head of the Bay of Puans, and a region thickly settled with Winnebagoes and Pottawotomies between the bay and Winnebago Lake, Sacs on Fox River, and Mascoutins, Kickapoos, and Miamis. Fox River, which they followed from the head of the bay, and of which the lake seemed only an expansion, was a rocky stream. A later traveler has told us that Fox River in its further extent is very crooked, and while seeming wide, with a boundary of hills on each hand, it affords but a slender channel in a marsh full of rushes and wild oats.

The Kickapoos and Mascoutins were rude, coarse-featured Indians. Though the missionary exhorted them as seriously as he did their gentler neighbors, he could not help remarking to Jolliet that "the Miamis were better made, and the two long earlocks which they wore gave them a good appearance."

It was the seventh day of June when the explorers arrived in this country of cabins woven of rushes ; and they did not linger here. Frenchmen had never gone farther. They were to enter new lands untrodden by the white race. They were in what is now called the state of Wisconsin, where "the soil was good," they noted, "producing much corn ; and the Indians gathered also quantities of plums and grapes." In these warmer lands the season progressed rapidly.

Marquette and Jolliet called the chiefs together and told them that Jolliet was sent by the governor to find new countries, and Marquette had been commissioned of Heaven to preach. Making the chiefs a present, without which they would not have received the talk seriously, the explorers asked for guides to that tributary which was said to run into the great river.

The chiefs responded with the gift of a rush mat for Marquette and Jolliet to rest on during their journey, and sent two young Miamis with them. If these kindly Indians disliked to set the expedition further on its way, they said nothing but very polite things about the hardi-

hood of Frenchmen, who could venture with
only two canoes, and seven in their party, on
unknown worlds.

The young Miamis, in a boat of their own,
led out the procession the tenth morning of
June. Taking up paddles, the voyageurs looked
back at an assembled multitude — perhaps the
last kindly natives on their perilous way — and
at the knoll in the midst of prairies where hospitable rush houses stood and would stand until
the inmates took them down and rolled them
up to carry to hunting grounds, and at groves
dotting those pleasant prairies where guests were
abundantly fed.

Three leagues up the marshy and oats-choked
Fox River, constantly widening to little lakes
and receding to a throat of a channel, brought
the explorers to the portage, or carrying place.
The canoes then had to be unloaded, and both
cargo and boats carried overland to a bend of
the Miscousing, which was the Indian name for
Wisconsin River. "This portage," says a traveler who afterwards followed that way, "is half
a league in length, and half of that is a kind of
marsh full of mud." In wet seasons the head
of Fox River at that time seemed not unlikely
to find the Wisconsin, for Marquette has set

it down in his recital that the portage was only
twenty-seven hundred paces.

When the two Miamis had helped to carry
the goods and had set the French on the tributary of the great river, they turned back to their
own country. Before the men entered the boats
Marquette knelt down with them on the bank
and prayed for the success of the undertaking.
It was a lovely broad river on which they now
embarked, with shining sands showing through
the clear water, making shallows like tumbling
discs of brilliant metal, — a river in which the
canoes might sometimes run aground, but one
that deceived the eye pleasantly, with islands all
vine covered, so when a boat clove a way between
two it was a guess how far the Wisconsin spread
away on each side to shores of a fertile land.
Oaks, walnuts, whitewood, and thorn trees
crowded the banks or fell apart, showing prairies rolling to wooded hills. Deer were surprised, stretching their delicate necks down to
drink at the margin. They looked up with shy
large eyes at such strange objects moving on
their stream, and shot off through the brush
like red-brown arrows tipped with white. The
moose planted its forefeet and stared stolidly,
its broad horns set in defense.

" Sieur Jolliet," said the missionary, once when the canoes drew together, " we have now left the waters which flow into the great lakes and are discharged through the St. Lawrence past Quebec to the sea. We follow those that lead us into strange lands."

" This river Miscousing on which we now are," returned Jolliet, " flows, as we see by our compass, to the southwestward. We know it is a branch of the great river. I am becoming convinced, Father, that the great river cannot discharge itself toward the east, as some have supposed."

The explorers estimated the distance from the country of the Mascoutins to the portage to be three leagues, and from the portage to the mouth of the Miscousing forty leagues. This distance they covered in a week. Drawing their canoes to the shore at night, they pitched camp, varying the monotony of their stores with fish and game. Perhaps they had learned that wild grapes then budding were not really fit to eat until touched by frost. Pierre Porteret said in Marquette's hearing, " the Indians could make good wine of grapes and plums if they desired."

The 17th of June, exactly one month from the day on which they had left St. Ignace mission, the explorers paddled into a gentle clear river, larger than the Miscousing but not yet monstrous in width, which ran southward. High hills guarded the right-hand shore, and the left spread away in fair meadows. Its current was broken with many little islands, like the Miscousing, though on sounding, Jolliet found the water to be ten fathoms, or sixty feet, deep. The shores receding, and then drawing in, gave unequal and irregular width to the stream. But it was unmistakably the great river they had sought, named then as now by the Indians, Mississippi, though Marquette at once christened it Conception, and another Frenchman who came after him gave it the name of Colbert. It was the river of which Nicollet had brought hints from his wanderings among northwestern tribes : the great artery of the middle continent, or, as that party of explorers believed, of the entire west. Receiving into itself tributaries, it rolled, draining a mighty basin, to unknown seas.

The first white men ventured forth upon its upper channel in two birch canoes. Five hardy voices raised a shout which was thrown back in an echo from the hills : five caps were whirled as high as paddles could raise them. But Marquette said, "This is such joy as we cannot express!" The men in both canoes silenced themselves while he gave thanks for the discovery.

FATHER JACQUES MARQUETTE.

From a Statue in the Capitol at Washington.

II.

BEARERS OF THE CALUMET.

Moving down the Mississippi, league after
league, the explorers noted first of all its solitude. Wigwam smoke could not be seen on
either shore. Silence, save the breathing of
the river as it rolled on its course, seemed to
surround and threaten them with ambush.
Still, day after day, the sweet and awful presence of the wilderness was their only company.
Once Pierre Porteret dropped his paddle with a
yell which was tossed about by echoing islands.
A thing with a tiger's forehead and a wildcat's
whiskered snout, holding ears and entire gray
and black head above the water, swam for the
boat. But it dived and disappeared ; and the
other voyageurs felt safe in laughing at him.
Not long after, Jacques bellowed aloud as he
saw a living tree glide under the canoe, jarring
it from end to end. The voyageurs soon learned
to know the huge sluggish catfish. They also
caught plenty of sturgeon or shovel fish when
they cast in their nets.

19

The river descended from its hilly cradle to
a country of level distances. The explorers,
seeing nothing of men, gave more attention
to birds and animals. Wild turkeys with burnished necks and breasts tempted the hunters.
The stag uttered far off his whistling call of
defiance to other stags. And they began to see
a shaggy ox, humped, with an enormous head
and short black horns, and a mane hanging over
low-set wicked eyes. Its body was covered with
curly rough hair. They learned afterwards from
Indians to call these savage cattle pisikious,
or buffaloes. Herds of many hundreds grazed
together, or, startled, galloped away, like thun-
der rolling along the ground.

The explorers kindled very little fire on shore
to cook their meals, and they no longer made a
camp, but after eating, pushed out and anchored,
sleeping in their canoes. Every night a senti-
nel was set to guard against surprise. By the
25th of June they had passed through sixty
leagues of solitude. The whole American continent was thinly settled by native tribes, many
in name indeed, but of scant numbers. The
most dreaded savages in the New World were
the Iroquois or Five Nations, living south of
Lake Ontario. Yet they were never able to

muster more than about twenty-two hundred fighting men.

The canoes were skirting the western bank, driven by the current, when one voyageur called to another:

" My scalp for the sight of an Indian ! "

" Halt ! " the forward paddler answered. " Look to thy scalp, lad, for here is the Indian! "

There was no feathered head in ambush, but they saw moccasin prints in the low moist margin and a path leading up to the prairie.

Marquette and Jolliet held the boats together while they consulted.

" Do you think it wise to pass by without searching what this may mean, Father? "

" No, I do not. We might thus leave enemies behind our backs to cut off our return. Some Indian village is near. It would be my counsel to approach and offer friendship."

" Shall we take the men? " debated Jolliet. " Two of them at least should stay to guard the canoes."

" Let them all stay to guard the canoes. If we go unarmed and unattended, we shall not raise suspicion in the savages' minds."

" But we may raise suspicion in our own minds."

Marquette laughed.

" The barbarous people on this unexplored river have us at their mercy," he declared. " We can at best do little to defend ourselves."

" Let us reconnoitre," said Jolliet.

Taking some of the goods which they had brought along for presents, Jolliet bade the men wait their return and climbed the bank with the missionary. The path led through prairie grass, gay at that season with flowers. The delicate buttercup-like sensitive plant shrank from their feet in wet places. Neither Frenchman had yet seen the deadly rattlesnake of these southern countries, singing as a great fly might sing in a web, dart out of its spotted spiral to fasten a death bite upon a victim. They walked in silence, dreading only the human beings they were going to meet. When they had gone about two leagues, the path drew near the wooded bank of a little stream draining into the Mississippi which they had scarcely noticed from the canoes. There they saw an Indian village, and farther off, up a hill, more groups of wigwams. They heard the voices of children, and nobody suspected their approach.

Jolliet and Marquette halted. Not knowing

how else to announce their presence, they shouted
together as loud as they could shout. The savages ran out of their wigwams and darted about
in confusion until they saw the two motionless
white men. The long black cassock of Marquette had instant effect upon them. For their
trinkets and a few garments on their bodies
showed that they had trafficked with Euro-
peans.

Four old Indians, slowly and with ceremony,
came out to meet the explorers, holding up
curious pipes trimmed with many kinds of
feathers. As soon as they drew near, Marquette called out to them in Algonquin:

" What tribe is this?"

" The Illinois," answered the old man. Being
a branch of the great Algonquin family, which
embraced nearly all northern aboriginal nations,
with the notable exception of the Iroquois, these
people had a dialect which the missionary could
understand. The name Illinois meant "The
Men."

Marquette and Jolliet were led to the principal lodge. Outside the door, waiting for
them, stood another old Indian like a statue
of wrinkled bronze. For he had stripped himself to do honor to the occasion, and held up

his hands to screen his face from the sun, making graceful and dignified gestures as he greeted the strangers.

"How bright is the sun when you come to see us, O Frenchmen! Our lodges are all open to you."

The visitors were then seated in the wigwam, and the pipe, or calumet, offered them to smoke, all the Indians crowding around and saying :

Calumet.

"You do well to visit us, brothers."

Obliged to observe this peace ceremony. Marquette put the pipe to his lips, but Jolliet, used to the tobacco weed, puffed with a good will.

The entire village then formed a straggling procession, gazing at the Frenchmen, whom they guided farther to the chief's town. He also met them standing with a naked retinue at his door, and the calumet was again smoked.

The Illinois lodges were shaped like the rounded cover of an emigrant wagon, high, and very long, having an opening left along

the top for the escape of smoke. They were
made of rush mats, which the women wove,
overlapped as shingles on a framework of
poles. Rush mats also carpeted the ground,
except where fires burned in a row along the
middle. Each fire was used by two families
who lived opposite, in stalls made of blankets.
The ends of the lodge had flaps to shut out the
weather, but these were left wide open to the
summer sun. During visits of ceremony a guest
stood where he could be seen and heard by all
who could crowd into the wigwam. But when
the Illinois held important councils they made
a circular inclosure, and built a camp-fire in the
center. Many families and many fires filled a
long wigwam, though Jolliet and Marquette
were lodged with the chief, who had one for
himself and his household.

Whitening embers were sending threads of
smoke towards a strip of blue sky overhead
when the missionary stood up to explain his
errand in the crowded inclosure, dividing his
talk into four parts with presents. By the first
gift of cloth and beads he told his listeners that
the Frenchmen were voyaging in peace to visit
nations on the river. By the second he said:

"I declare to you that God, your Creator, has

pity on you, since, when you have been so long
ignorant of him, he wishes to become known to `
you. I am sent on his behalf with this design.
It is for you to acknowledge and obey him."

By the third gift they were informed that the
chief of the French had spread peace and over-
come the Iroquois. And the last begged for
all the information they could give about the
sea and intervening nations.

When Marquette sat down, the chief stood
up and laid his hand on the head of a little
slave, prisoner from another tribe.

"I thank you, Blackgown." he said, "and
you, Frenchman, for taking so much pains to
come and visit us. The earth has never been
so beautiful, nor the sun so bright, as to-day ;
never has the river been so calm and free from
rocks, which your canoes removed as they passed!
Never has our tobacco had so fine a flavor, nor
our corn appeared so beautiful as we find it
to-day. Here is my son. I give him to you
that you may know my heart. Take pity on
us and all our nation. You know the Great
Spirit who made all : you speak to him and
hear him : ask him to give us life and health
and come and dwell with us."

When the chief had presented his guests with

the Indian boy, and again offered the calumet,
he urged them, with belts and garters of
buffalo wool, brilliantly dyed, to go no farther
down the great river, on account of dangers.
These compliments being ended, a feast was
brought in four courses. First came a wooden
dish of sagamity or corn-meal boiled in water
and grease. The chief took a buffalo-horn
spoon and fed his guests as if they had been
little children ; three or four spoonfuls he put
in Marquette's mouth and three or four spoonfuls in Jolliet's. Three fish were brought next,
and he picked out the bones with his own fingers, blew on the food to cool it, and stuffed
the explorers with all he could make them
accept. It was their part to open their mouths
as young birds do. The third course was that
most delicate of Indian dishes, a fine dog ; but
seeing that his guests shrank from this, the
chief ended the meal with buffalo meat, giving them the fattest parts.

The Illinois were at that time on the west
side of the Mississippi, because they had been
driven from their own country on the Illinois
River by the Iroquois. The Illinois nation was
made up of several united tribes : Kaskaskias,
Peorias, Kahokias, Tamaroas, and Moingona.

Flight scattered them, and these were only a few of their villages. They afterwards returned to their own land. Their chief wore a scarf or belt of fur crossing his left shoulder, encircling his waist and hanging in fringe. Arm and leg bands ornamented him, and he also had knee rattles of deer hoofs. Paint made of colored clays streaked his face. This attractive creature sent the Indian crier around, beating a drum of deer hide stretched over a pot, to proclaim the calumet dance in honor of the explorers.

Marquette and Jolliet were led out in the prairie to a small grove which sheltered the assembly from the afternoon sun. Even the women left their maize fields and the beans, melons, and squashes that they were cultivating, and old squaws dropped rush braiding, and with papooses swarming about their knees, followed. The Illinois were nimble, well-formed people, skillful with bow and arrow. They had, moreover, some guns among them, obtained from allies who had roved and traded with the French. Young braves imitated the gravity of their elders at this important ceremony. The Illinois never ate new fruits or bathed at the beginning of summer, without first dancing the calumet.

A large gay mat of rushes was spread in the center of the grove, and the warrior selected to dance put his god, or manitou — some tiny carven image which he carried around his person and to which he prayed — on the mat beside a beautiful calumet. Around them he spread his bow and arrows, his war club, and

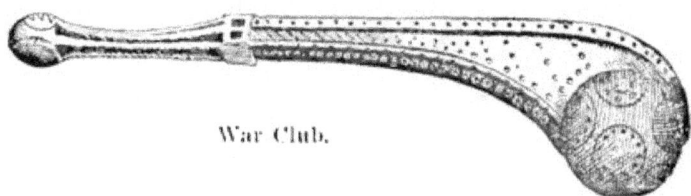

War Club.

stone hatchet. The pipe was made of red rock like brilliantly polished marble, hollowed to hold tobacco. A stick two feet long, as thick as a cane, formed the stem. For the dance these pipes were often decked with gorgeous scarlet, green, and iridescent feathers, though white plumes alone made them the symbol of peace, and red quills bristled over them for war.

Young squaws and braves who were to sing, sat down on the ground in a group near the mat ; but the multitude spread in a great circle around it. Men of importance before taking their seats on the short grass, each in turn lifted the calumet, which was filled, and blew a little

smoke on the manitou.   Then the dancer sprang
out, and, with graceful curvings in time to the
music, seized the pipe and offered it now to the
sun and now to the earth, made it dance from
mouth to mouth along the lines of spectators,
with all its fluttering plumes spread.   The hazy
sun shone slanting among branches, tracing a
network of flickering leaf shadows on short
grass ; and liquid young voices rising and falling chanted,

> " Nanahani, nanahani, nanahani,
>   Naniango ! "

The singers were joined by the Indian drum ;
and at that another dancer sprang into the

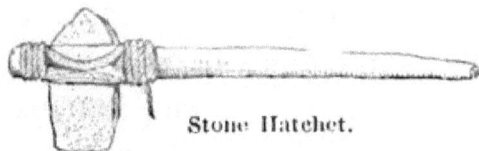

Stone Hatchet.

circle and took the weapons from the mat to
fight with the principal dancer, who had no
defense but the calumet.   With measured steps
and a floating motion of the body the two ad-
vanced and attacked, parried and retreated,
until the man with the pipe drove his enemy
from the ring.   Papooses of a dark brick-red
color watched with glistening black eyes the

last part of the dance, which celebrated victory.
The names of nations fought, the prisoners
taken, and all the trophies brought home were
paraded by means of the calumet.

The chief presented the dancer with a fine
fur robe when he ended; and, taking the calumet from his hand, gave it to an old man in the
circle. This one passed it to the next, and so
it went around the huge ring until all had held
it. Then the chief approached the white men.

"Blackgown," he said, "and you, Frenchman, I give you this peace-pipe to be your safe-
guard wherever you go among the tribes. It
shall be feathered with white plumes, and dis-
playing it you may march fearlessly among
enemies. It has power of life and death, and
honor is paid to it as to a manitou. Blackgown, I give you this calumet in token of peace
between your governor and the Illinois, and to
remind you of your promise to come again and
instruct us in your religion."

The explorers slept soundly all night in the
chief's lodge, feeling as safe as among Christian
Indians of the north, who stuck thorns in a
calendar to mark Sundays and holydays. Next
morning the chief went with several hundred
of his people to escort them to their canoes;

but it was three o'clock in the afternoon before
the voyageurs, dropping down stream, saw the
last of the friendly tribe.

Day after day the boats moved on without
meeting other inhabitants. Mulberries, per-
simmons, and hazelnuts were found on the
shores. They passed the mouth of the Illinois
River without knowing its name, or that it
flowed through lands owned by the tribe that
had given them the peace-pipe. Farther on,
the Mississippi made one of its many bends,
carrying them awhile directly eastward, and
below great rocks like castles. As the canoes
ran along the foot of this east shore, some of
the voyageurs cried out. For on the face of the
cliff far up were two painted monsters in glaring
red, green, and black; each as large as a calf,
with deer horns, blood-colored eyes, tiger beard,
a human face, and a body covered with scales.
Coiled twice around the middle, over the head,
and passing between the hind legs of each,
extended a tail that ended like a fish. So
startling was this sight, which seemed a banner
held aloft heralding unseen dangers, that the
men felt threatened by a demon. But Marquette laughed at them and beckoned for the
canoes to be brought together.

"What manner of thing is this, Sieur Jolliet?"

"A pair of manitous, evidently. If we had Indians with us, we should see them toss a little tobacco out as an offering in passing by."

"I cannot think," said Marquette, "that any Indian has been the designer. Good painters in France would find it hard to do as well. Besides this, the creatures are so high upon the rock that it was hard to get conveniently at them to paint them. And how could such colors be mixed in this wilderness?"

"We have seen what pigments and clays the Illinois used in daubing themselves. These wild tribes may have among them men with natural skill in delineating," said Jolliet.

"I will draw them off," Marquette determined, bringing out the papers on which he set down his notes; and while the men stuck their paddles in the water to hold the canoes against the current, he made his drawing.

One of the monsters seen by the explorers remained on those rocks until the middle of our own century. It was called by the Indians the Piasa. More than two centuries of beating winter storms had not effaced the brilliant picture when it was quarried away by a stupidly

barbarous civilization. The town of Alton, in
the state of Illinois, is a little south of that rock
where the Piasa dragons were seen.

As the explorers moved ahead on glassy
waters, they looked back, and the line of vision
changing, they saw that the figures were cut
into the cliff and painted in hollow relief.

They were still talking about the monsters
when they heard the roar of a rapid ahead, and
the limpid Mississippi turned southward on its
course. It was as if they had never seen the
great river until this instant. For a mighty
flood, rushing through banks from the west,
yellow with mud, noisy as a storm, eddying
islands of branches, stumps, whole trees, took
possession of the fair stream they had followed
so long. It shot across the current of the Mississippi in entering so that the canoes danced
like eggshells and were dangerously forced to
the eastern bank. Afterwards they learned
that this was the Pekitanoüi, or, as we now
call it, the Missouri River, which flows into the
Mississippi not far above the present city of St.
Louis; and that by following it to its head
waters and making a short portage across a
prairie, a man might in time enter the Red or
Vermilion Sea of California.

Having slipped out of the Missouri's reach,
the explorers were next threatened by a whirlpool among rocks before they reached the mouth
of Ouaboukigou, the Ohio River. They saw
purple, red, and violet earths, which ran down
in streams of color when wet, and a sand which
stained their paddles like blood. Tall canes
began to feather the shore, and mosquitoes
tormented them as they pressed on through
languors of heat. Jolliet and Marquette made
awnings of sails which they had brought as a
help to the paddles. They were floating down
the current of the muddy, swollen river when
they saw Indians with guns on the east shore.
The voyageurs dropped their paddles and seized
their own weapons. Marquette stood up and
spoke to the Indians in Huron. They made no
answer. He held up the white calumet. Then
they began to beckon, and when the party drew
to land, they made it clear that they had themselves been frightened until they saw the Blackrobe holding the calumet. A long-haired tribe,
somewhat resembling the Iroquois, but calling
themselves Tuscaroras; they were rovers, and
had axes, hoes, knives, beads, and double glass
bottles holding gunpowder, for which they had
traded with white people eastward.

They fed the French with buffalo meat and white plums, and declared it was but a ten days' journey to the sea. In this they were mistaken, for it was more than a thousand miles to the Gulf of Mexico.

To each tribe as he passed, Marquette preached his faith by the belt of the prayer. For each

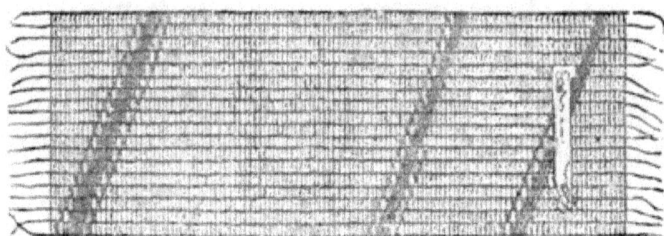

Wampum Girdle.

he had a wampum girdle to hold while he talked, and to leave for a remembrance. His words without a witness would be forgotten.

Three hundred miles farther the explorers ventured, and had nearly reached the mouth of the Arkansas River, floating on a wide expanse of water between lofty woods, when they heard wild yelling on the west shore, and saw a crowd of savages pushing out huge wooden canoes to surround them. Some swam to seize the Frenchmen, and a war club was thrown over their heads. Marquette held up the peace-pipe, but the wild young braves in the water paid no

attention to it. Arrows were ready to fly from
all sides, and Marquette held the peace-pipe
on high and continually prayed. At once old
Indians restrained the young ones. In their
turmoil they had not at first seen the calumet;
but two chiefs came directly out to bring the
strangers ashore.

Not one of the missionary's six languages was
understood by these Indians. He at last found
a man who spoke a little Illinois, and Jolliet
and he were able to explain their errand. He
preached by presents, and obtained a guide to
the next nation.

On that part of the river where the French
came to a halt, the Spanish explorer De Soto
was said to have died two hundred years before.
In this region the Indians had never seen snow,
and their land yielded three crops a year. Their
pots and plates were of baked earth, and they
kept corn in huge gourds, or in baskets woven
of cane fibers. They knew nothing of beaver
skins; their furs were the hides of buffaloes.
Watermelons grew abundantly in their fields.
Though they had large wigwams of bark, they
wore no clothing, and hung beads from their
pierced noses and ears.

These Akamsea, or Arkansas Indians showed

traits of the Aztecs under Spanish dominion;
for what is now the state of Texas was then
claimed by Spain. Marquette and Jolliet held
a council. They were certain that the great
river discharged itself into the Gulf of Mexico.
If they ventured farther, they might fall into
the hands of Spaniards, who would imprison
them; or they might be killed by fiercer tribes
than any yet encountered, and in either case
their discoveries would be lost. So they decided
to turn back.

All day the Arkansas feasted them with
merciless savage hospitality, and it was not
polite to refuse food or the attention of rock-
ing. Two stout Indians would seize a voyageur
between them and rock him back and forth for
hours. If the motion nauseated him, that was
his misfortune.

Pierre Porteret crept out behind one of the
bark lodges looking very miserable in the fog of
early morning. His companion on many a long
journey, never far out of his shadow, sat down
to compare experiences.

"Did they rock thee all night, Pierre?"

"They rocked me all night, Jacques. I can
well endure what most men can, but this is
carrying politeness too far."

"I was not so favored. They would have saved you if they had killed the rest of us. And they would have saved the good father, no doubt, since the chief came and danced the calumet before him."

"Were these red cradle-rockers intending to make an end of us in the night?"

"So the chief says; but he broke up the council, and will set us safely on our journey up river to-day."

"I am glad of that," said Pierre. "Father Marquette hath not the strength of the Sieur Jolliet for such rude wanderings. These southern mists, and torturing insects, and clammy heats, and the bad food have worked a great change in him."

"We have been gone but two months from the Mission of St. Ignace," said Jacques. "They have the bigness of years."

"And many more months that have the bigness of years will pass before we see it again."

They grew more certain of this, when, after toiling up the current through malarial nights and sweltering days, the explorers left the Mississippi and entered the river Illinois. There, above Peoria Lake, another Illinois town of seventy-four lodges was found, and these Kas-

kaskias so clung to the Blackrobe that he
promised to come back and teach them. From
the head waters of the Illinois a portage was
made to Lake Michigan, and the French returned
to the Bay of the Puans alongshore. They had
traveled over twenty-five hundred miles, and
accomplished the object of their journey.

Jolliet, with his canoe of voyageurs, his maps
and papers, and the young Indian boy given
him by the Illinois chief, went on to Montreal.
His canoe was upset in the rapids of Lachine
just above Montreal, and he lost two men, the
Indian boy, his papers, and nearly everything
except his life. But he was able to report to
the governor all that he had seen and done.

Marquette lay ill, at the Bay of the Puans, of
dysentery, brought on by hardship; and he was
never well again. Being determined, however,
to go back and preach to the tribe on the Illinois
River, he waited all winter and all the next summer to regain his strength. He carefully wrote
out and sent to Canada the story of his discoveries and labors. In autumn, with Pierre Porteret and the voyageur Jacques, he ventured
again to the Illinois. Once he became so ill
they were obliged to stop and build him a cabin
in the wilderness, at the risk of being snowed

in all winter. It was not until April that he
reached what he called his Mission of the
Immaculate Conception, on the Illinois River,
through snow, and water and mud, hunger and
misery. He preached until after Easter, when,
his strength being exhausted, Pierre and Jacques
undertook to carry him home to the Mission of
St. Ignace. Marquette had been two years
away from his palisaded station on the north
shore, and nine years in the New World.

It was the 19th of May, and Pierre and
Jacques were paddling their canoe along the
east side of that great lake known now as
Michigan. A creek parted the rugged coast,
and dipping near its shallow mouth they looked
anxiously at each other.

"What shall we do?" whispered Jacques.

"We must get on as fast as we can," answered
Pierre.

They were gaunt and weather-beaten themselves from two years' tramping the wilderness.
But their eyes dwelt most piteously on the dying
man stretched in the bottom of the canoe. His
thin fingers held a cross. His white face and
bright hair rested on a pile of blankets. Pierre
and Jacques felt that no lovelier, kinder being
than this scarcely breathing missionary would

ever float on the blue water under that blue
sky.

He opened his eyes and saw the creek they
were slipping past, and a pleasant knoll beside
it, and whispered: —

"There is the place of my burial."

"But, Father," pleaded Pierre, "it is yet
early in the day.   We can take you farther."

"Carry me ashore here," he whispered again.

So they entered the creek and took him
ashore, building a fire and sheltering him as
well as they could.   There a few hours afterward he died, the weeping men holding up his
cross before him, while he thanked the Divine
Majesty for letting him die a poor missionary.
When he could no longer speak, they repeated
aloud the prayers he had taught them.

They left him buried on that shore with a
large cross standing over his grave.   Later his
Indians removed his bones to the Mission of St.
Ignace, with a procession of canoes and a priest
intoning.   They were placed under the altar of
his own chapel.   If you go to St. Ignace, you
may see a monument now on that spot, and
people have believed they traced the foundation
of the old bark chapel.   But the spot where he
first lay was long venerated.

A great fur trader and pioneer named Gurdon Hubbard made this record about the place, which he visited in 1818 : —

" We reached Marquette River, about where the town of Ludington now stands on the Michigan shore. This was where Father Marquette died, about one hundred and forty years before, and we saw the remains of a red-cedar cross, erected by his men at the time of his death to mark his grave; and though his remains had been removed to the Mission, at Point St. Ignace, the cross was held sacred by the voyageurs, who, in passing, paid reverence to it, by kneeling and making the sign of the cross. It was about three feet above the ground, and in a falling condition. We reset it, leaving it out of the ground about two feet, and as I never saw it after, I doubt not that it was covered by the drifting sands of the following winter, and that no white man ever saw it afterwards."

III.

THE MAN WITH THE COPPER HAND.

ONE day at the end of August, when Marquette's bones had lain under his chapel altar nearly two years and a half, the first ship ever seen upon the lakes was sighted off St. Ignace. Hurons and Ottawas, French traders, and coureurs de bois, or wood-rangers, ran out to see the huge winged creature scudding betwixt Michilimackinac Island and Round Island. She was of about forty-five tons' burden. Five cannon showed through her portholes, and as she came nearer, a carved dragon was seen to be her figurehead; she displayed the name Griffin and bore the white flag of France. The priest himself felt obliged to receive her company, for three Récollet friars, in the gray robe of St. Francis, appeared on the deck. But two men, one in a mantle of scarlet and gold, and the other in white and gold French uniform, were most watched by all eyes.

The ship fired a salute, and the Indians howled with terror and started to run; then

THE BUILDING OF THE GRIFFIN.

From the Original Engraving in Father Hennepin's "Nouvelle Découverte," Amsterdam, 1704.

turned back to see her drop her sails and her anchor, and come up in that deep crescent-shaped bay. She had weathered a hard storm in Lake Huron; but the men who handled her ropes were of little interest to coureurs de bois on shore, who watched her masters coming to land.

"It is the Sieur de la Salle in the scarlet mantle," one coureur de bois said to another. "And this is the ship he

La Salle.

hath been building at Niagara. First one hears that creditors have seized his fort of Fronte-nac, and then one beholds him sailing here in state, as though naught on earth could daunt him."

"I would like service with him," said the other coureur de bois.

His companion laughed.

"Service with La Salle means the hardest

marching and heaviest labor a voyageur ever undertook. I have heard he is himself tough as iron. But men hereabouts who have been in his service will take to the woods when they hear he has arrived; traders that he sent ahead with goods. If he gets his hand on them after he finds they have squandered his property, it will go hard with them."

" He has a long gray-colored face above his broad shoulders. I have heard of this Sieur Robert Cavelier de la Salle ever since he came to the province more than ten years ago, but I never saw him before. Is it true that Count Frontenac is greatly bound to him?"

"So true that Sieur de la Salle thereby got favor at court. It was at court that a prince recommended to him yon swart Italian in white and gold that he brought with him on his last voyage from France. Now, there is a man known already throughout the colony by reason of his hand."

" Which hand?"

" The right one."

" I see naught ailing that. He wears long gauntlets pulled well over both wrists."

" His left hand is on his sword hilt. Doth he not hold the right a little stiffly? "

"It is true. The fingers are not bent."

"They never will be bent. It is a hand of copper."

"How can a man with a copper hand be of service in the wilderness?"

The first ranger shrugged. "That I know not. But having been maimed in European wars and fitted with a copper hand, he was yet recommended to Sieur de la Salle."

"But why hath an Italian the uniform of France?"

"He is a French officer, having been exiled with his father from his own country."

The coureur de bois, who had reached the settlement later than his companion, grunted.

"One would say thou wert of the Griffin crew thyself, with the latest news from Quebec and Montreal."

"Not I," laughed the first one. "I have only been in the woods with Greysolon du Lhut, who knows everything."

"Then he told thee the name of this Italian with the copper hand?"

"Assuredly. This Italian with the copper hand is Sieur Greysolon du Lhut's cousin, and his name is Henri de Tonty."

"I will say this for Monsieur Henri de

Tonty: a better made man never stepped on the strand at St. Ignace."

Greysolon du Lhut was the captain of coureurs de bois in the northwest. No other leader had

Autograph of Tonty.

such influence with the lawless and daring. When these men were gathered in a settlement, spending what they had earned in drinking and gaming, it was hard to restrain them within civilized bounds. But when they took service to shoulder loads and march into the wilderness, the strongest hand could not keep them from open rebellion and desertion. There were few devoted and faithful voyageurs, such as Pierre Porteret and Jacques had proved themselves in following Marquette. The term of service was usually two years; but at the first hardship some might slip away in the night, even at the risk of perishing before they reached the settlements.

St. Ignace made a procession behind La Salle's party and followed them into the chapel to hear mass — French traders, Ottawas, Hurons, coureurs de bois, squaws, and children. When the priest turned from the altar, he looked down on complexions ranging from the natural pallor of

La Salle to the black-red of the most weather-beaten native.

The Hurons then living at St. Ignace, whom Father Marquette had led there from his earlier mission, after-wards wandered to Detroit and Sandusky, the priests having decided to aban-don St. Ignace and burn the chapel. In our own day we hear of their descend-ants as settled in

Totem of the Hurons.

the Indian Territory, the smallest but wealthiest band of all transplanted Indians.

Having entered the lake region with impressive ceremonies, which he well knew how to employ before ignorant men and savages, La Salle threw aside his splendor, and, with his lieutenant, put on the buckskins for marching and canoe journeying into the wilderness. Some of the men he had sent up the lakes with goods nearly a year before had collected a large store of furs, worth much money; and these he de-

termined to send back to Canada on the Griffin,
to satisfy his creditors and to give him means
for carrying on his plans.   He had meant, after
sending Tonty on to the Illinois country, to
return to Canada and settle his affairs.   But
it became necessary, as soon as he landed at
St. Ignace, to divide his party and send Tonty
with some of the men to Sault Ste. Marie after
plunderers who had made off with his goods.
The others would doubtless desert if left any
length of time without a leader.   It was a risk
also to send his ship back to the colony without
standing guard over its safety himself.   But he
greatly needed the credit which its load of furs
would give him.   So he determined to send it
manned as it was, with orders to return to the
head of Lake Michigan as soon as the cargo was
safely landed ; while he voyaged down the west
side of the lake, and Tonty, returning from the
Sault, came by the east shore.   The reunited
party would then have the Griffin as a kind of
floating fort or refuge. and by means of it keep
easily in communication with the settlements.

La Salle wanted to build a chain of forts from
Niagara to the mouth of the Mississippi, when
that could be reached.   Around each of these,
and protected by them, he foresaw settlements

of French and Indians, and a vast trade in furs
and the products of the undeveloped west. Thus
France would acquire a province many times its
own size. The undertaking was greater than
conquering a kingdom. Nobody else divined at
that time the wonderful promise of the west as
La Salle pictured it. Little attention had been
paid to the discoveries of Marquette and Jolliet.
France would have got no benefit from them
had not La Salle so soon followed on the track
of missionary and trader, verified what had been
done, and pushed on.

He had seen Jolliet twice. The first time
they met near Niagara, when both were exploring; the second time, Jolliet is said to have
stopped with his maps and papers before they
were lost at Fort Frontenac, on his return from
his Mississippi voyage. La Salle, then master
of Fort Frontenac, must have examined these
charts and journals with interest. It does not
appear that the two men were ever very friendly.
Jolliet was too easily satisfied to please La
Salle; he had not the ability to spread France's
dominion over the whole western wilderness,
and that was what La Salle was planning to
do before Marquette and Jolliet set out for the
Mississippi.

St. Ignace became once more the starting point of an important expedition, though La Salle, before sending the Griffin back, sailed in her as far as the Bay of Puans, where many of his furs were collected. He parted with this good ship in September. She pointed her prow eastward, and he turned south with fourteen men in four canoes, carrying tools, arms, goods, and even a blacksmith's forge.

Through storm, and famine, and peril with Indians they labored down the lake, and did not reach the place where they were to meet Tonty until the first of November. La Salle had the three Récollet friars with him. Though one was a man sixty-four years old, he bore, with his companions, every hardship patiently and cheerfully. The story of priests who helped to open the wilderness and who carried religion to savages is a beautiful chapter of our national life.

Tonty was not at the place where they were to meet him. This was the mouth of the St. Joseph River, which La Salle named the Miamis. The men did not want to wait, for they were afraid of starving if they reached the Illinois country after the Indians had scattered to winter hunting grounds. But La Salle would not go on until Tonty appeared. He put the men to work building a timber stockade, which he called Fort Miamis; thus beginning in the face of discouragement his plan of creating a line of fortifications.

Tonty, delayed by lack of provisions and the need of hunting, reached Fort Miamis with his men in twenty days. But the Griffin did not come at all. More than time enough had passed for her to reach Fort Niagara, unload her cargo, and return. La Salle watched the lake constantly for her sails. He began to be heavy-hearted for her, but he dared wait no longer; so, sending two men back to meet and guide her to this new post, he moved on.

Eight canoes carried his party of thirty-three people. They ascended the St. Joseph River to find a portage to the head waters of the Illinois. This brought them within the present state of Indiana: and when they had reached that curve of the river where South Bend now stands, they left St. Joseph to grope for the Theakiki, or Kankakee, a branch called by some Indians the Illinois itself.

La Salle became separated from the party on this portage, eagerly and fearlessly scouring the woods for the river's beginning. Tonty camped and waited for him, fired guns, called, and

searched; but he was gone all night and until
the next afternoon. The stars were blotted
overhead, for a powder of snow thickened the
air, weirdly illuminating naked trees in the darkness, but shutting in his vision. It was past
midnight when he came in this blind circle once
more to the banks of the St. Joseph, and saw a
fire glinting through dense bushes.

"Now I have reached camp," thought La
Salle, and he fired his gun to let his people know
he was approaching. Echoes rolled through the
woods. Without waiting for a shot in reply he
hurried to the fire. No person was near it. The
descending snow hissed, caught in the flames.
Here was a home hearth prepared in the wilderness, and no welcome to it but silence. La Salle
called out in every Indian language he knew.
Dead branches grated, and the stream rustled
betwixt its edges of ice. A heap of dry grass
was gathered for a bed under a tree by the fire,
and its elastic top showed the hollow where a
man had lain. La Salle put some more wood
on the fire, piled a barricade of brush around the
bed, and lay down in a place left warm by some
strolling Indian whom his gun had frightened
away. He slept until morning. In the afternoon he found his own camp.

From the first thread of the Kankakee oozing out of swamps to the Indian town on the Illinois River where Marquette had done his last missionary work, was a long canoe journey. It has been said the rivers of the New World made its rapid settlement possible; for they were open highways, even in the dead of winter guiding the explorer by their frozen courses.

The Illinois tribe had scattered to their hunting, and the lodges stood empty. La Salle's men were famished for supplies, so he ventured to open the covered pits in which the Indians stored their corn. Nothing was more precious than this hidden grain; but he paid for what he took when he reached the Indians. This was not until after New Year's day. He had descended the river as far as that expansion now called Peoria Lake.

The Illinois, after their first panic at the appearance of strange white men, received La Salle's party kindly, fed all with their own fingers, and, as they had done with Jolliet and Marquette when those explorers passed them on the Mississippi, tried to coax their guests to go no farther. They and other Indians who came to the winter camp told such tales of danger on that great river about which the French knew

so little, that six of La Salle's men deserted in
one night.

This caused him to move half a league beyond
the Illinois camp, where, on the southern bank,
he built a palisaded fort and called it Crèvecœur.
He was by this time convinced that the Griffin
was lost.   Whether she went down in a storm,
or was scuttled and sunk by those to whom he
intrusted her, nothing was ever heard of her
again.   The furs he had sent to pay his creditors never in any way reached port.   If they
escaped shipwreck, they were stolen by the men
who escaped with them.

Nothing could bend La Salle's resolution.   He
meant in some way to explore the west through
which the southern Mississippi ran.   But the
loss of the Griffin hurt him sorely.   He could
not go on without more supplies; and having
no vessel to bring them, the fearful necessity
was before him of returning on foot and by
canoe to Fort Frontenac to bring them himself.

He began to build another ship on the Illinois
River, and needed cables and rigging for her.
This vessel being partly finished by the first of
March, he left her and Fort Crèvecœur in
Tonty's charge, and, taking four Frenchmen

and a Mohegan hunter, set out on the long and terrible journey to Fort Frontenac.

The Italian commandant with the copper hand could number on its metal fingers the only men to be trusted in his garrison of fifteen. One Récollet, Father Louis Hennepin, had been sent with two companions by La Salle to explore the upper Mississippi. Father Ribourde and Father Membré remained. The young Sieur de Boisrondet might also be relied on, as well as a Parisian lad named Étienne Renault, and their servant L'Esperance. As for the others, smiths, shipwrights, and soldiers were ready to mutiny any moment. They cared nothing about the discovery of the west. They were afraid of La Salle when he was with them; and, though it is said no man could help loving Tonty, these lawless fellows loved their own wills better.

The two men that La Salle had sent to look for the Griffin arrived at Fort Crèvecœur, bearing a message from him, having met him on the way. They had no news, but he wrote a letter and sent them on to Tonty. He urged Tonty to take part of the garrison and go and fortify a great rock he had noticed opposite the Illinois town. Whatever La Salle wanted done Tonty was anxious to accomplish, though separating

himself from Crèvecœur, even for a day, was a
dangerous experiment. But he took some men
and ascended the river to the rock. Straight-
way smiths, shipwrights, and soldiers in Crèvecœur, seizing powder, lead, furs, and provisions,
deserted and made their way back to Canada.
Boisrondet, the friars, and L'Esperance hurried
to tell Tonty; and thus Fort Crèvecœur and
the partly finished ship had to be abandoned.
Tonty dispatched four men to warn La Salle of
the disaster. He could neither hold this posi-
tion nor fortify the rock in the midst of jealous
savages with two friars, one young officer, a lad,
and one servant. He took the forge, and tools,
and all that was left in Crèvecœur into the very
heart of the Indian village and built a long
lodge, shaped like the wigwams of the Illinois.
This was the only way to put down their suspicion. Seeing that the Frenchmen had come
to dwell among them, the Indians were pleased,
and their women helped with poles and mats to
build the lodge.

For by this time, so long did it take to cover
distances in the wilderness, spring and summer
were past, and the Illinois were dwelling in their
great town, nearly opposite the rock which La
Salle desired to have fortified. Tonty often

gazed at it across the river, which flows southwestward there, with a ripple that does not break
into actual rapids. The yellow sandstone height,
rising like a square mountain out of the shore,
was tufted with ferns and trees. No man could
ascend it except at the southeast corner, and at
that place a ladder or a rope was needed by the
unskillful. It had a flat, grassy top shut in by
trees, through which one could see the surrounding country as from a tower. A ravine behind
it was banked and floored with dazzling white
sand, and walled at the farther side by a timbered
cliff rising to a prairie. With a score of men
Tonty could have held this natural fortress
against any attack. Buckets might be rigged
from overhanging trees to draw up water from
the river. Provisions and ammunition only
were needed for a garrison. This is now called
Starved Rock, and is nearly opposite the town of
Utica. Some distance up the river is a longer
ridge, yet known as Buffalo Rock, easy of ascent
at one end, up which the savages are said to have
chased buffaloes ; and precipitous at the other,
down which the frightened beasts plunged to
death.

The tenth day of September a mellow autumn
sun shone on maize fields where squaws labored,

on lazy old braves sprawled around buffalo robes,
gambling with cherry stones, and on peaceful
lodges above which the blue smoke faintly
wavered.   It was so warm the fires were nearly
out.   Young warriors of the tribes were away
on an expedition; but the populous Indian town
swarmed with its thousands.

Father Ribourde and Father Membré had
that morning withdrawn a league up the river
to make what they called a retreat for prayer
and meditation.   The other Frenchmen were
divided between lodge and garden.

Near this living town was the town of the
dead, a hamlet of scaffolds, where, wrapped in
skins, above the reach of wolves, Illinois Indians
of a past generation slept their winters and
summers away.   Crows flapped across them
and settled on the corn, causing much ado
among the papooses who were set to shout
and rattle sticks for the protection of the crop.

Suddenly a man ran into camp, having just
leaped from the canoe which brought him across
the river.   When he had talked an instant old
braves bounded to their feet with furious cries,
the tribes flocked out of lodges, and women and
children caught the panic and came screeching.

"What is the matter?" exclaimed Tonty,

unable to understand their rapid jargon. The Frenchmen drew together with the instinct of uniting in peril, and, led by old men, the Indian mob turned on them.

" What is it?" cried Tonty.

" The Iroquois are coming! The Iroquois are coming to eat us up! These Frenchmen have brought the Iroquois upon us!"

" Will you stand off!" Tonty warned them. And every brave in the town knew what they called the medicine hand in his right gauntlet, powerful and hard as a war club. They stood in awe of it as something more than human. He put his followers behind him. The French-men crowded back to back, facing the savage crowd. Hampered by his imperfect knowledge of their language, he hearkened intently to the jangle of raging voices, his keen dark eyes sweeping from face to face. Tonty was a man of impressive presence, who inspired confidence even in Indians. They held back from slaying him and his people, but fiercely accused him. Young braves dragged from the French lodge the goods and forge saved from Fort Crèvecœur, and ran yelling to heave everything into the river.

" The Iroquois are your friends! The Iroquois

are at peace with the French! But they are
marching here to eat us up!"

"We know nothing about the Iroquois!"
shouted Tonty. "If they are coming we will
go out with you to fight them!"

Only half convinced, but panic-stricken from
former encounters with a foe who always drove
them off their land, they turned from threatening Tonty and ran to push out their canoes.
Into these were put the women and children,
with supplies, and all were paddled down river
to an island, where guards could be set. The
warriors then came back and prepared for fighting. They greased their bodies, painted their
faces, made ready their weapons, and danced
and howled to excite one another to courage.
All night fires along shore, and leaping figures,
were reflected in the dark river.

About dawn, scouts who had been sent to
watch the Iroquois came running with news
that the enemy were almost in sight across the
prairie on the opposite side, slipping under cover
of woods along a small branch of the Illinois
River. They had guns, pistols, and swords, and
carried bucklers of rawhide. The scouts declared
that a Jesuit priest and La Salle himself led
them.

The Frenchmen's lives seemed hardly a breath long. In the midst of maddened, screeching savages Tonty and his men once more stood back to back, and he pushed off knives with his copper hand.

"Do you want to kill yourselves?" he shouted. "If you kill us, the French governor will not leave a man of you alive! I tell you Monsieur de la Salle is not with the Iroquois, nor is any priest leading them! Do you not remember the good Father Marquette? Would such men as he lead tribes to fight one another? If all the Iroquois had stolen French clothes, you would think an army of Jesuits and Messieurs de la Salle were coming against you!"

"But some one has brought the Iroquois upon us!"

"I told you before we know nothing about the Iroquois! But we will go with you now to fight them!"

At that the Illinois put their knives in their belts and ran shouting to throw themselves into the canoes. Warfare with American Indians .was always the rush of a mob, where every one acted for himself without military order.

"It is well the good friars are away making their retreat," said Tonty to Boisrondet and

Étienne Renault while they paddled as fast as they could across the river with the Illinois. "Poor old L'Esperance must be making a retreat, too."

"I have not myself seen him since last night," Boisrondet remembered.

"He put out in a canoe when the Indians were embarking their women and children," said Étienne Renault. "I saw him go."

And so it proved afterwards. But L'Esperance had slipped away to bring back Father Membré and Father Ribourde to tend the wounded and dying.

Having crossed the river and reached the prairie, Tonty and his allies saw the Iroquois.

Long House of the Iroquois.

They came prancing and screeching on their savage march, and would have been ridiculous if they had not been appalling. These Hodeno-saunee, or People of the Long House, as they called themselves, were the most terrible force in the New World. Tonty saw at once it would go hard with the Illinois nation. Never at any time as hardy as their invaders, who by frequent attacks had broken their courage, and weakened by the absence of their best warriors, they wavered in their first charge.

He put down his gun and offered to carry a peace belt to the Iroquois to stop the fight. The Illinois gladly gave him a wampum girdle and sent a young Indian with him. Boisrondet and Étienne Renault also walked at his side into the open space between two barbaric armies. The Iroquois did not stop firing when he held up and waved the belt in his left hand. Bullets spattered on the hummocky sod of the prairie around him.

"Go back," Tonty said to Boisrondet and Renault and the young Indian. "What need is there of so many? Take the lad back, Boisrondet."

They hesitated to leave him

"Go back!" he repeated sharply, so they turned, and he ran on alone. The Iroquois guns seemed to flash in his face. It was like throwing himself among furious wolves. Snarling lips and snaky eyes and twisting sinuous

bodies made nightmares around him. He felt
himself seized; a young warrior stabbed him
in the side. The knife glanced on a rib, but
blood ran down his buckskins and filled his
throat.

"Stop!" shouted an Iroquois chief. "This
is a Frenchman; his ears are not pierced."

Tonty's swarthy skin was blanching with the
anguish of his wound, which turned him faint.
His black hair clung in rings to a forehead wet
with cold perspiration. But he held the wampum belt aloft and spat the blood out of his
mouth.

"Iroquois! The Illinois nation are under the
protection of the French king and Governor
Frontenac! I demand that you leave them
in peace!"

A young brave snatched his hat and lifted it
on the end of a gun. At that the Illinois began
a frenzied attack. thinking he was killed. Tonty
was spun around as in a whirlpool. He felt a
hand in his hair and a knife at his scalp.

"I never," he thought to himself, "was in
such perplexity in my life!"

"Burn him!" shouted some.

"But he is French!" others cried. "Let
him go!"

Through all the uproar he urged the peace belt and threatened them with France. The wholesome dread which Governor Frontenac had given to that name had effect on them. Besides, they had not surprised the Illinois, and if they declared a truce, time would be gained to consider their future movements.

The younger braves were quieted, and old warriors gave Tonty a belt to carry back to the Illinois. He staggered across the prairie. Father Ribourde and Father Membré, who had just reached the spot, ran to meet him, and supported him as he half fainted from loss of blood.

Tonty and his allies withdrew across the river. But the Iroquois, instead of retreating, followed. Seeing what must happen, Tonty thought it best for the Illinois to give up their town and go to protect their women and children, while he attempted as long as possible to keep the invaders at bay. Lodges were set on fire, and the Illinois withdrew quietly down river, leaving some of their men in the bluffs less than a league from the town, to bring them word of the result. The Frenchmen, partially rebuilding their own lodge, which had been wrecked when their goods were thrown in the river, stood their ground in the midst of insulting savages.

For the Iroquois, still determined on war and despoiling, opened maize pits, scattering and burning the grain; trampled corn in the fields; and even pulled the dead off their scaffolds. They were angry at the French for threatening them with that invisible power of France, and bent on chasing the Illinois. Yet Tonty was able to force a kind of treaty between them and the retreating nation. through the men left in the bluffs. As soon as they had made it, however, they began canoes of elm bark, to follow the Illinois down river.

Two or three days passed, while the Frenchmen sat covering the invaded tribe's retreat. They scarcely slept at night. Their enemies prowled around their lodge or celebrated dances on the ruins of the town. The river flowed placidly, and the sun shone on desolation and on the unaltered ferny buttresses of the great rock and its castellated neighbors. Tonty heard with half delirious ears the little creatures which sing in the grass and fly before man, but return to their singing as soon as he passes by. The friars dressed and tended his fevered wound, and when the Iroquois sent for him to

come to a council, Father Membré went with
him.

Within the rude fort of posts and poles saved
from ruined lodges, which the Iroquois had
built for themselves, adding a ruff of freshly
chopped trees, the two white men sat down in
a ring of glowering savages. Six packs of
beaver skins were piled ready for the oration ;
and the orator rose and addressed Tonty.

With the first two the Indian spokesman
promised that his nation would not eat Count
Frontenac's children, those cowardly Illinois.

The next was a plaster to heal Tonty's
wound.

The next was oil to anoint him and the
Récollets, so their joints would move easily
in traveling.

The next said that the sun was bright.

And the sixth and last pack ordered the
French to get up and leave the country.

When the speaker sat down, Tonty came
to his feet and looked at the beaver skins
piled before them.   Then he looked around the
circle of hard weather-beaten faces and restless eyes, and thanked the Iroquois for their
gift.

"But I would know," said Tonty, "how soon

you yourselves intend to leave the country and let the Illinois be in peace?"

There was a growl, and a number of the braves burst out with the declaration that they intended to eat Illinois flesh first.

Tonty raised his foot and kicked the beaver skins from him. In that very way they would have rejected a one-sided treaty themselves. Up they sprang with drawn knives and drove him and Father Membré from the fort.

All night the French stood guard for fear of being surprised and massacred in their lodge. At daybreak the chiefs ordered them to go without waiting another hour, and gave them a leaky boat.

Tonty had protected the retreat of the Illinois as long as he could. With the two Récollets, Boisrondet, young Renault, and L'Espérance, and with little else, he set out up the river.

IV.

THE UNDESPAIRING NORMAN.

"THE northward current of the eastern shore of Lake Michigan and the southward current of the western shore," says a writer exact in knowledge, "naturally made the St. Joseph portage a return route to Canada, and the Chicago portage an outbound one." But though La Salle was a careful observer and must have known that what was then called the Chekago River afforded a very short carrying to the Desplaines or upper Illinois, he saw fit to use the St. Joseph both coming and going.

His march to Fort Frontenac he afterwards described in a letter to one of the creditors interested in his discoveries.

"Though the thaws of approaching spring greatly increased the difficulty of the way, interrupted as it was everywhere by marshes and rivers, to say nothing of the length of the journey, which is about five hundred leagues in a direct line, and the danger of meeting Indians of four or five different nations, through whose

country we were to pass, as well as an Iroquois
army which we knew was coming that way;
though we must suffer all the time from hunger;
sleep on the open ground, and often without
food; watch by night and march by day, loaded
with baggage, such as blanket, clothing, kettle,
hatchet, gun, powder, lead, and skins to make
moccasins; sometimes pushing through thickets,
sometimes climbing rocks covered with ice and
snow; sometimes wading whole days through
marshes where the water was waist deep or even
more, — all this did not prevent me from going
to Fort Frontenac to bring back the things we
needed and to learn myself what had become of
my vessel."

Carrying their canoes where the river was
frozen, and finally leaving them hidden near
where the town of Joliet now stands, La Salle
and his men pushed on until they reached the
fort built at the mouth of the St. Joseph. Here
he found the two voyageurs he had sent to
search for the Griffin. They said they had been
around the lake and could learn nothing of
her. He then directed them to Tonty, while
he marched up the eastern shore. This Michigan region was debatable ground among the
Indians, where they met to fight; and he left

significant marks on the trees, to make prowlers
think he had a large war party. A dozen
or twenty roving savages, ready to pounce like
ferocious wildcats on a camp, always peeled
white places on the trees, and cut pictures there
of their totem, or tribe mark, and the scalps
and prisoners they had taken. They respected
a company more numerous than themselves,
and avoided it.

Stopping to nurse the sick when some fell ill
of exposure, or to build canoes when canoes
were needed, La Salle did not reach Fort Niagara until Easter, and it was May when Fort
Frontenac came into view.

No man ever suffered more from treachery.
Before he could get together the supplies he
needed, trouble after trouble fell upon him.
The men that Tonty had sent to tell him about
the destruction of Fort Crèvecœur were followed
by others who brought word that the deserters
had destroyed his forts at the St. Joseph River
and Niagara, and carried off all the goods. The
Griffin was certainly lost. And before going
back to the Illinois country he was obliged to
chase these fellows and take from them what
could be recovered. But when everybody else
seemed to be against him, it was much comfort

to remember he had a faithful lieutenant while the copper-handed Italian lived.

La Salle gathered twenty-five men of trades useful to him, and another outfit with all that he needed for a ship, having made new arrangements with his creditors; and going by way of Michilimackinac, he reached the St. Joseph early in November.

Whenever, in our own day, we see the Kankakee still gliding along its rocky bed, or the solemn Illinois spreading betwixt wooded banks, it is easy to imagine a birch canoe just appearing around a bend, carrying La Salle or Tonty, and rowed by buckskin-clad voyageurs. On the Kankakee thousands of buffaloes filled the plains, and La Salle's party killed many, preparing the flesh in dried flakes by smoking it.

The buffaloes were left behind when they approached the great town on the Illinois. La Salle glanced up at the rock he wanted fortified, but no palisade or Frenchman was to be seen.

" It seems very quiet," he said to the men in his canoe, " and we have not passed a hunter. There — there is the meadow where the town stood : but where is the town ? "

Heaps of ashes, charred poles, broken scaffolds, wolves prowling where papooses had

played, crows whirling in black clouds or
sitting in rows on naked branches, bones, —
a horrible waste plain had taken the place of
the town.

The Frenchmen scattered over it, eagerly
seeking some trace of Tonty and his companions. They labored all day, until the sun set,
among dreadful sights which they could never
forget, without finding any clue to his fate.

They piled charred wood together and made
a fire and camped among ruins. But La Salle
lay awake all night, watching the sharp-pointed
autumn stars march overhead, and suffering
what must have seemed the most unendurable
of all his losses.

Determined not to give up his friend, he rose
next morning and helped the men hide their
heavy freight in the rocks, leaving two of them
to hide with and guard it, and went on down
the Illinois River. On one bank the retreat of
the invaded tribe could be traced, and on the
other the dead camp-fires of the Iroquois who
had followed them. But of Tonty and his
Frenchmen there was still no sign.

La Salle saw the ruins of Fort Crèvecœur and
his deserted vessel. And so searching he came
to the mouth of the Illinois and saw for the first

time that river of his ambitions, the Mississippi.
There he turned back, leaving a letter tied to a
tree, on the chance of its sometime falling into
the hands of Tonty. There was nothing to do
but to take his men and goods from among the
rocks near the destroyed town and return to
Fort Miamis, on the St. Joseph, which some of
his followers had rebuilt. The winter was upon
them.

La Salle never sat and brooded over trouble.
He was a man of action. Shut in with his men
and goods, and obliged to wait until spring
permitted him to take the next step, he began
at once to work on Indian hunters, and to draw
their tribes towards forming a settlement around
the rock he meant to fortify on the Illinois.
Had he been able to attach turbulent voyageurs
to him as he attached native tribes, his heroic
life would have ended in success even beyond
his dreams. Tonty could better deal with
ignorant men, his military training standing
him in good stead; yet Tonty dared scarcely
trust a voyageur out of his sight.

While Tonty and La Salle were passing
through these adventures, the Récollet father,
Louis Hennepin, and his two companions, sent
by La Salle, explored the upper Mississippi.

One of these was named Michael Ako; the other, Du Gay, a man from Picardy in France.

They left Fort Crèvecœur on the last day of February, twenty-four hours before La Salle started northward, and entered the Mississippi on the 12th of March. The great food-stocked stream afforded them plenty of game, wild turkeys, buffaloes, deer, and fish. The adventurers excused themselves from observing the Lenten season set apart by the Church for fasting; but Father Hennepin said prayers several times a day. He was a great robust Fleming, with almost as much endurance as that hardy Norman, La Salle.

They had paddled about a month up river through the region where Marquette and Jolliet had descended, when one afternoon they stopped to repair their canoe and cook a wild turkey. Hennepin, with his sleeves rolled back, was daubing the canoe with pitch, and the others were busy at the fire, when a war whoop, followed by continuous yelling, echoed from forest to forest, and a hundred and twenty naked Sioux or Dacotah Indians sprang out of boats to seize them. It was no use for Father Hennepin to show a peace-pipe or offer fine tobacco. The Frenchmen were prisoners. And when these

savages learned by questioning with signs, and
by drawing on the sand with a stick, that the
Miamis, whom they were pursuing to fight, were

far eastward out of
their reach, three or
four old warriors laid
their hands on Hen-
nepin's shaven crown
and began to cry and
howl like little boys.

The friar in his
long gray capote or
h o o d e d garment,
which fell to his feet,

Totem of the Sioux.

girt about the waist
by a rope called the cord of St. Francis, stood,
with bare toes showing on his sandals, inclin-
ing his fat head with sympathy. He took out
his handkerchief and wiped the old men's faces.
Du Gay and Ako, in spite of the peril, laughed
to see him daub the war paint.

"The good father hath no suspicion that
these old wretches are dooming him to death,"
said Ako to Du Gay.

It appeared afterwards that this was what the
ceremony meant. For several days the Frenchmen, carried northward in their captors' boats,

expected to die. No calumet was smoked with
them; and every night one of the old chiefs,
named Aquipaguetin, who had lost a son in war
and formed a particular intention of taking
somebody's scalp for solace, sat by the prisoners
stroking them and howling by the hour. One
night when the Frenchmen were forced to make
their fire at the end of the camp, Aquipaguetin
sent word that he meant to finish them without
more delay. But they gave him some goods
out of the store La Salle had sent with them,
and he changed his mind and concluded to wait
awhile. He carried the bones of one of his dead
relations, dried and wrapped in skins gaily ornamented with porcupine-quill work; and it was
his custom to lay these bones before the tribe and
request that everybody blow smoke on them. Of
the Frenchmen, however, he demanded hatchets,
beads, and cloth. This cunning old Sioux wanted
to get all he could before the party reached
their villages, where the spoil would be divided.

Nineteen days after their capture the prisoners were brought to a place which is now the
site of St. Paul in the state of Minnesota, where
the Sioux disbanded, scattering to their separate
towns. They had finally smoked the peace-
pipe with the Frenchmen; and now, fortunately

without disagreement, portioned their white
captives and distributed the goods. Father
Hennepin was given to Aquipaguetin, who
promptly adopted him as a son. The Flemish
friar saw with disgust his gold-embroidered
vestments, which a missionary always carried
with him for the impressive celebration of
mass, displayed on savage backs and greatly
admired.

The explorers were really in the way of seeing
as much of the upper Mississippi as they could
desire. They were far north of the Wisconsin's
mouth, where white men first entered the great
river. The young Mississippi, clear as a mountain stream, gathered many small tributaries.
St. Peter's joined it from a blue-earth channel.
This rugged northern world was wonderfully
beautiful, with valleys and heights and rocks
and waterfalls.

The Sioux were tall, well-made Indians, and
so active that the smaller Frenchmen could
hardly keep up with them on the march. They
sometimes carried Du Gay and Ako over streams,
but the robust friar they forced to wade or swim;
and when he lagged lame-footed with exhaus-
tion across the prairies, they set fire to grass
behind him, obliging him to take to his heels

with them or burn. By adoption into the family of Aquipaguetin he had a large relationship thrust upon him, for the old weeper had many wives and children and other kindred. Hennepin indeed felt that he was not needed and might at any time be disposed of. He never had that confidence in his father Aquipaguetin which a son should repose in a parent.

He was separated from Ako and Du Gay, who were taken to other villages. By the time he reached father Aquepaguetin's house he was so exhausted, and his legs, cut by ice in the streams, were so swollen that he fell down on a bear robe. The village was on an island in a sheet of water afterwards called Lake Buade. Hennepin was kindly received by his new family, who fed him as well as they were able, for the Sioux had little food when they were not hunting. Seeing him so feeble, they gave him an Indian sweating bath, which he found good for his health. They made a lodge of skins so tight that it would hold heat, and put into it stones baked to a white heat. On these they poured water and shut Hennepin in the steam until he sweated freely.

The Sioux had two kinds of lodges — one somewhat resembling those of the Illinois, the

other a cone of poles with skins stretched
around, called a tepee.

Father Hennepin did little missionary work
among these Indians. He suffered much from
hunger, being a man who loved good cheer. But
the tribes went on a buffalo hunt in July and
killed plenty of meat. All that northern world
was then clothed in vivid verdure. Honey-
suckles and wild grapevines made the woods
fragrant. The gentian, which jealously closes
its blue-fringed cup from the human eye, grew
close to the lakes. Captive though the Frenchmen were, they could not help enjoying the
evening camp-fire with its weird flickerings
against the dark of savage forests, the heat-
lightning which heralded or followed storms,
the waters, clear, as if filtered through icebergs,
dashing in foam over mossy rocks.

They met during the buffalo hunt, and it
was about this time that some "spirits," or white
men, were heard of, coming from Lake Superior.
These proved to be the great ranger Greysolon
du Lhut and four other Frenchmen.

This man, cousin to Tonty, passed nearly his
whole life in the woods, going from Indian town
to Indian town, or planting outposts of his
own in the wilderness. Occasionally he went to

France, and the king's magnificence at Versailles was endured by him until he could gain some desired point from the colonial minister and hurry back. The government relied on him to keep lawless coureurs de bois within bounds, and he traded with nearly all the western tribes. When Greysolon du Lhut appeared, the Sioux treated their prisoners with deference; and from that time Hennepin, Du Gay, and Ako went where they pleased.

They seemed to have had no thought of returning to Fort Crèvecœur. In those days when each man took his individual life in his hands and guarded it in ways which seemed best to him, it was often expedient to change one's plan of action. About the time that Tonty was obliged to abandon Fort Crèvecœur, Hennepin and his companions set off eastward with Greysolon du Lhut's party. Hennepin sailed for France as soon as he could and wrote a book about his adventures. It was one of La Salle's misfortunes that this friar should finally even lay claim to discovering the mouth of the Mississippi, adding the glory of that to these real adventures on its upper waters.

The first of March, La Salle, with a number of the men he had gathered, started from Fort

Miamis to the Illinois country. The prairies were one dazzling expanse of snow, and as the party slid along on the broad, flat snowshoes to which their feet were strapped, some of them were so blinded that the pain in their eyes became unendurable. These were obliged to camp in the edge of some woods, while the rest went on.

La Salle himself was sitting in darkness while the spring sun struck a million sparkles from a world yet locked in winter. The wind chilled his back, and he spread his hands to the camp blaze. In the torment of snow-blindness he wondered whether Tonty was treading these white wastes, seeking him, or lying dead of Indian wounds under the snow crust. The talk of the other snow-blinded men, sitting about or stretched with their feet to the fire, was lost on his ear. Yet his one faithful servant, who went with him on all his journeys, could not see anything but calm fortitude on his face as he lifted it at the approach of snowshoes.

"I cannot see you, Hunaut," said La Salle. " Did you find some pine leaves?"

"I found some, monsieur."

" Steep them as soon as you can for the men's eyes."

"I wish to tell you, monsieur," the man said as he went about his task with a snow-filled kettle, "that I found also a party of Fox Indians from Green Bay, and they gave me news of Monsieur de Tonty."

Hunaut looked at the long, pale face of his master and saw the under lip tremble and twitch.

"You know I am much bound to Monsieur de Tonty. Is he alive?"

"He is alive, monsieur. He has been obliged to pass the winter at Green Bay. Father Hennepin has also passed through that country on his way to Montreal."

La Salle felt his troubles melt with the unlocking of winter. The brief but agonizing snow-blindness passed away with a thaw; and, overtaking his other men, he soon met the returning Illinois tribe and began the Indian settlement around the rock he intended to fortify.

Already the Miami tribe was following him, and he drew them into an alliance with the Illinois, impressively founding the principality soon to grow there. This eloquent Norman Frenchman had gifts in height and the large bone and sinew of Normandy, which his Indian allies always admired. And he well knew where to impress his talk with coats, shirts, guns, and hunting-knives. As his holdings of land in Canada were made his stepping-stones toward the west, so the footing he gained at Fort Miamis and in the Illinois country was to be used in discovering the real course of the Mississippi and taking possession of its vast basin.

It was the end of May before he met Tonty at St. Ignace; Italian and Frenchman coming together with outstretched arms and embracing. Tonty's black eyes were full of tears, but La Salle told his reverses as calmly as if they were another man's.

"Any one else," said Father Membré, who stood by, "would abandon the enterprise, but Monsieur de la Salle has no equal for constancy of purpose."

"But where is Father Ribourde?" La Salle inquired, missing the other Récollet.

Tonty told him sorrowfully how Father Ribourde had gone into the woods when his party camped, after being driven up river in a leaky boat by the Iroquois; how they had waited and searched for him, and were finally made aware that a band of prowling Kickapoos had murdered him.

Tonty had aimed at Green Bay by the Chicago portage, and tramped along the west shore of Lake Michigan, having found it impossible to patch the boat.

"We were nearly starved," he said; "but we found a few ears of corn and some frozen squashes in a deserted Indian town. When we reached the bay we found an old canoe and mended it; but as soon as we were on the water there rose a northwest wind with driving snow, which lasted nearly five days. We ate all our food, and, not knowing what to do, turned back to the deserted town to die by a warm fire in one of the wigwams. On the way the bay froze. We camped to make moccasins out of Father Membré's cloak. I was angry at Étienne Renault for not finishing his; but he excused himself on account of illness, having a great oppression of the stomach, caused by eating a piece of an Indian rawhide shield which he could not digest. His delay proved our salvation, for the next day, as I was urging him to finish the moccasins, a party of Ottawas saw the smoke of our fire and came to us. We gave them such a welcome as never was seen before. They took us into their canoes and carried us to an Indian village only two leagues off. All the Indians took pleasure in sending us food ; so, after thirty-four days of starvation, we found our famine turned to abundance."

Tonty and La Salle, with their followers, paddled the thousand miles to Fort Frontenac, to make another start into the wilderness.

La Salle was now determined to keep his men together. He set down many of his experiences and thoughts in letters which have been kept; so we know at this day what was in the great explorer's mind, and how dear he held "Monsieur de Tonty, who is full of zeal."

On his return to the wilderness with another equipment, he went around the head of Lake Michigan and made the short Chicago portage to the Desplaines River. Entering by this branch the frozen Illinois, they dragged their canoes on sledges past the site of the town and reached open water below Peoria Lake. La Salle gave up the plan of building a ship, and determined to go on in his canoes to the mouth of the Mississippi.

So, pausing to hunt when game was needed, his company of fifty-four persons entered the great river, saw the Missouri rushing into it — muddy current and clear northern stream flowing alongside until the waters mingled. They

met and overawed the Indians on both shores,
building several stockades. The broad river
seemed to fill a valley, doubling and winding
upon itself with innumerable curves, in its
solemn and lonely stretches. Huge pieces of
low-lying bank crumbled and fell in with
splashes, for the Mississippi ceaselessly eats
away its own shore.

A hundred leagues below the mouth of the
Arkansas they came to a swamp on the west
side. Behind this swamp, they had been told,
might be found the Arkansas tribe's great town.
La Salle sent Tonty and Father Membré, with
some voyageurs, to make friends with the
Indians and bring him word about the town.

Tonty had seen nothing like it in the New
World. The houses were large and square, of
sun-baked brick, with a dome of canes overhead.
The two largest were the chief's house and the
temple. Doors were the only openings. Tonty
and the friar were taken in where the chief sat
on a bedstead with his squaws, and sixty old
men, in white mulberry bark cloaks, squatted
by with the dignity of a council. The wives,
in order to honor the sovereign, yelled.

The temple was a place where dead chiefs'
bones were kept. A mud wall built around it

was ornamented with skulls. The inside was very rough. Something like an altar stood in the center of the floor; and a fire of logs was kept burning before it, and never allowed to go out, filling the place with smoke, and irritating the eyes of two old Indians who tended it in half darkness. The Frenchmen were not allowed to look into a secret place where the temple treasure was kept. But, hearing it consisted of pearls and trinkets, Tonty conjectured the Indians had got it from the Spanish. This tribe was not unlike the Aztecs of Mexico. The chief came in barbaric grandeur to visit La Salle, dressed in white, having fans carried before him, and a plate of burnished copper to represent the sun, for these lower Mississippians were sun-worshipers.

With gifts and the grave consideration which instantly won Indians, La Salle moved from tribe to tribe towards the Gulf. Red River pulsed upon the course like a discharging artery. The sluggish alligator woke from the ooze and poked up his snout at the canoes. "He is," says a quaint old writer who made that journey afterwards, "the most frightful master-fish that can be seen. I saw one that was as large as half a hogshead. There are some, they say, as large as

a hogshead and twelve to fifteen feet long. I
have no doubt they would swallow up a man if
they caught him."

In April La Salle reached his goal. He
found that the Mississippi divided its current
into three strands
and entered the Gulf
through three mouths.
He separated his
party; La Salle took
the west passage, and
Tonty and another
lieutenant the middle
and the east. At the
Gulf of Mexico they
came together again,
and with solemn cere-
monies claimed for
France all the country
along the great river's

La Salle
at the Mouth of the Mississippi.

entire length, and far eastward and westward,
calling it Louisiana, in honor of King Louis
XIV. A metal plate, bearing the arms of
France, the king's name, and the date of the
discovery, was fixed on a pillar in the shifting
soil.

Hardy as he was, La Salle sometimes fell ill

from the great exposures he endured. And more
than once he was poisoned by some revengeful
voyageur.   It was not until the December following his discovery of the Mississippi's mouth
that he realized his plan of fortifying the rock
on the Illinois River.   He and Tonty delighted
in it, calling it Fort St. Louis of the Illinois.
Storehouses and quarters for a garrison rose
around its edges, protected by a palisade.   A
windlass was rigged to draw water from the
river below.   On the northeast corner of the
rock a low earthwork remains to this day.

Around this natural castle the Indian tribes
gathered to La Salle, as to a sovereign, — Miamis,
Abenakis, and Shawanoes, from countries eastward, and the Illinois returned to spread over
their beloved meadow.   Instead of one town,
many towns of log, or rush, or bark lodges
could be seen from the summit of the Rock.
Years afterwards the French still spoke of this
fortress as Le Rocher.   A little principality of
twenty thousand inhabitants, strong enough to
repel any attack of the Iroquois, thus helped to
guard it.   La Salle meant to supply his people
with goods and give them a market for their
furs.   At this time he could almost see the success of his mighty enterprise assured; he could

reasonably count on strengthening his stockades along the Mississippi, and on building near its mouth a city which would protect the entire west and give an outlet to the undeveloped wealth of the continent.

In the flush of his discovery and success La Salle went back to France, leaving Tonty in charge of the Rock and the gathering Indian nations, and laid his actual achievements before the king, asking for help. This was made necessary by the change in the colonial government, which had re-

Louis XIV., King of France.

moved his friend Count Frontenac and left him at the mercy of enemies.

The king was not slow to see the capacity of

this wonderful man, so shy of civilization that
he lodged in a poor street, carrying with him
the very breath of the wilderness.   La Salle
asked for two ships; the king gave him four;
and many people and supplies were gathered to
colonize and stock the west.

It was La Salle's intention to sail by way of
the West Indies, cross the Gulf of Mexico, and
enter the mouth of the Mississippi.   But the
Gulf of Mexico is rimmed with low marshy
land, and he had never seen the mouth of the
Mississippi from seaward.   His unfamiliarity
with the coast, or night, or fog cheated him of
his destination, and the colony was landed four
hundred miles west of it, in a place called Mata-
gorda Bay, in Texas, which then belonged to
the Spaniards.   Although at the time of discovery he had taken the latitude of that exact
spot where he set the post, he had been unable
to determine the longitude; any lagoon might
be an opening of the triple mouth he sought.

La Salle's brother, a priest, who sailed with
him on this voyage, testified afterwards that
the explorer died believing he was near the
mouth of the Mississippi.   Whatever may have
been his thoughts, the undespairing Norman
grappled with his troubles in the usual way.

One of his vessels had been captured by the
Spanish. Another had been wrecked in the
bay by seamen who were willing to injure him.
These contained supplies most needed for the
colony. The third sailed away and left him;
and his own little ship, a gift of the king for
his use along the coast, was sunk by careless
men while he was absent searching northward
for the Mississippi.

Many of the colonists fell sick and died. Men
turned sullen and tried to desert. Some went
hunting and were never seen again. Indians,
who dare not openly attack, skulked near and
set the prairie on fire; and that was a sight of
magnificence, the earth seeming to burn like a
furnace, or, far as the eye could follow them,
billows of flame rushing as across a fire sea.
But La Salle was wise, and cut the grass close
around his powder and camp.

Water, plains, trees combined endlessly, like
the pieces of a kaleidoscope, to confuse him in
his search. Tonty was not at hand to take care
of the colony while he groped for the lost river.
He moved his wretched people from their camp,
with all goods saved off the wreck in the bay,
to a better site for a temporary fort, on rising
ground. The carpenters proved good for noth-

ing. La Salle himself planned buildings and marked out mortises on the logs. First a large house roofed with hides, and divided into apartments, was finished to shelter all. Separate

La Salle's Map of Texas.

houses were afterwards built for the women and girls, and barracks or rougher cells for the men. A little chapel was finally added. And when high-pointed palisades surrounded the whole, La Salle, perhaps thinking of his invincible rock

on the Illinois and the faithfulness of his copper-
handed lieutenant guarding it, called this outpost also Fort St. Louis. Cannon were mounted
at the four corners of the large house. As the
balls were lost, they were loaded with bullets
in bags.

Behind, the prairies stretched away to forests.
In front rolled the bay, with the restless ever-
heaving motion of the Mexican Gulf. A delicious salty air, like the breath of perpetual spring,
blew in, tingling the skin of the sulkiest adventurer with delight in this virgin world. Fierce
northers must beat upon the colonists, and the
languors of summer must in time follow ; and
they were homesick, always watching for sails.
Yet they had no lack of food. Oysters were
so plentiful in the bay that they could not
wade without cutting their feet with the shells.
Though the alligator pushed his ugly snout and
ridgy back out of lagoons, and horned frogs
frightened the children, and the rattlesnake was
to be avoided where it lay coiled in the grass,
game of all kinds abounded. Every man was
obliged to hunt, and every woman and child to
help smoke the meat. Even the priests took guns
in their hands. Father Membré had brought
some buffalo traditions from the Illinois coun-

try. He was of Father Hennepin's opinion that this wild creature might be trained to draw the plow, and he had faith that benevolence was concealed behind its wicked eyes.

As Father Membré stalked along the prairie with the hunters, his capote tucked up out of his way on its cord, one of the men shot a buffalo and it dropped. The buffaloes rarely fell at once, even when wounded to death, unless hit in the spine. Father Membré approached it curiously.

"Come back, Father!" shouted the hunters.

Father Membré touched it gently with his gun.

"Run, Father, run!" cried the hunters.

"It is dead," asserted Father Membré. "I will rest my gun across its carcass to steady my aim at the other buffaloes."

He knelt to rest his gun across its back.

The great beast heaved convulsively to its feet and made a dash at the Récollet. It sent him revolving heels over head. But Father Membré got up. and, spreading his capote in both hands, danced in front of the buffalo to head it off from escaping. At that, with a bellow, the shaggy creature charged over him across the prairie, dropping to its knees and dying before the frightened hunters could lift the friar from the ground.

"Are you hurt, Father?" they all asked, supporting him, and finding it impossible to keep from laughing as he sat up, with his reverend face skinned and his capote nearly torn off.

"Not unto death," responded Father Membré, brushing grass and dirty hoof prints from his garment. "But it hath been greatly impressed on my mind that this ox-savage is no fit beast for the plow. Nor will I longer counsel our women to coax the wild cows to a milking. It is well to adapt to our needs the beasts of a country," said Father Membré, wiping blood from his face. "But this buffalo creature hath disappointed me!"

La Salle was prostrated through the month of November. But by Christmas he was able to set out on a final search from which he did not intend to return until he found the Mississippi. All hands in the fort were busied on the outfit necessary for the party. Clothes were made of sails recovered from one of the wrecked vessels. Eighteen men were to follow La Salle, among them his elder brother, the Abbé Cavelier. Some had on the remains of garments they had worn in France, and others were dressed in deer or

buffalo skins. He had bought five horses of
the Indians to carry the baggage.

At midnight on Christmas Eve everybody
crowded into the small fortress chapel. The
priests, celebrating mass, moved before the altar
in such gold-embroidered vestments as they had,
and the light of torches illuminated the rough
log walls. Those who were to stay and keep
the outpost, literally lost in the wilderness, were
on their knees weeping. Those who were to go
knelt also, with the dread of an awful uncer-
tainty in their minds. The faithful ones foresaw
worse than peril from forests and waters and
savages, for La Salle could not leave behind all
the villains with whom he was obliged to serve
himself. He alone showed the composure of a
man who never despairs. If he had positively
known that he was setting out upon a fatal
journey, — that he was undertaking his last
march through the wilderness, — the mass lights
would still have shown the firm face of a man
who did not turn back from any enterprise.
The very existence of these people who had
come out to the New World with him depended
on his success. Whatever lay in the road he
had to encounter it. The most splendid lives
may progress and end through what we call

tragedy; but it is better to die in the very stress of achievement than to stretch a poor existence through a century. The contagion of his hardihood stole out like the Christmas incense and spread through the chapel.

V.

FRENCH SETTLEMENTS.

"IT was the establishment of military posts throughout this vast valley that eventually brought on a life struggle between the English and the French," says a historian.

At first the only spot of civilization in boundless wilderness was Tonty's little fort on the Illinois. Protected by it, the Indians went hunting and brought in buffalo skins and meat; their women planted and reaped maize; children were born; days came and went; autumn haze made the distances pearly; winter snow lay on the wigwams; men ran on snowshoes; and papooses shouted on the frozen river. Still no news came from La Salle.

Tonty had made a journey to the mouth of the Mississippi to meet him, after he landed with his colony, searching thirty leagues in each direction along the coast. La Salle was at that time groping through a maze of lagoons in Texas. Tonty, with his men, waded swamps to their necks, enduring more suffering than

MAP OF THE FRENCH SETTLEMENTS.

he had ever endured in his life before. This
was in February of the year 1686. Finding
it impossible to reach La Salle, who must be
wandering somewhere on the Gulf of Mexico,
Tonty wrote a letter to him, intrusting it to the
hands of an Indian chief, with directions that it
be delivered when the explorer appeared. He
also left a couple of men who were willing to
wait in the Arkansas villages to meet La Salle.

Two years passed before those men brought
positive proof of the undespairing Norman's
fate. The remnant of the party that started
with La Salle from Fort St. Louis of Texas
spent one winter at Fort St. Louis of the
Illinois, bringing word that they had left their
leader in good health on the coast. The Abbé
Cavelier even collected furs in his brother's
name, and went on to France, carrying his
secret with him.

La Salle had been assassinated on the Trinity
River, soon after setting out on his last determined search for the Mississippi. The eight-
eenth day of March, 1687, some of his brutal
voyageurs hid themselves in bushes and shot
him.

So slowly did events move then, and so
powerless was man, an atom in the wilderness,

that the great-hearted Italian, weeping aloud in rage and grief, realized that La Salle's bones had been bleaching a year and a half before the news of his death reached his lieutenant. It was not known that La Salle received burial. The wretches who assassinated him threw him into some brush. It was a satisfaction to Tonty that they all perished miserably afterwards; those who survived quarrels among themselves being killed by the Indians.

The undespairing Norman died instantly, without feeling or admitting defeat. And he was not defeated. Though his colony — including Father Membré, who had been so long with him — perished by the hands of the Indians in Texas, in spite of Tonty's second journey to relieve them, his plan of settlements from the great lakes to the mouth of the Mississippi became a reality.

Down from Canada came two of the eleven Le Moyne brothers, D'Iberville and Bienville, fine fighting sons of a powerful colonial family, with royal permission to found near the great river's mouth that city which had been La Salle's dream. Fourteen years after La Salle's death, while D'Iberville was exploring for a site, the old chief, to whom Tonty had given a letter for La Salle, brought it carefully wrapped and delivered it into the hands of La Salle's more fortunate successor.

Tonty was associated with Le Moyne D'Iberville in these labors around the Gulf.

Autograph of Le Moyne D'Iberville.

A long peninsula betwixt the Mississippi and Kaskaskia Rivers, known since as the American Bottom, lured away Indians from the great town on the Illinois. The new settlement founded on this peninsula was called Kaskaskia, for one of the tribes. As other posts sprung into existence, Fort St. Louis was less needed. "As early as 1712," we are told, "land titles were issued for a common field in Kaskaskia. Traders had already opened a commerce in skins and furs with the remote post of Isle Dauphine in Mobile Bay." Settlements were firmly established. By 1720 the luxuries of Europe came into the great tract taken by La Salle in the name of King Louis and called Louisiana.

Twelve years after La Salle's death a missionary named St. Cosme (Saut' Come) journeyed from Canada in a party guided by Tonty. St. Cosme has left this record of the man with the copper hand : —

"He guided us as far as the Arkansas and gave us much pleasure on the way, winning friendship of some savages and intimidating others who from jealousy or desire to plunder opposed the voyage; not only doing the duty of a brave man but that of a missionary. He quieted the voyageurs, by whom he was generally loved, and supported us by his example in devotion."

On the Chicago portage a little boy, given to the missionary perhaps because he was an orphan and the western country offered him the best chances in life, started eagerly ahead, though he was told to wait. The rest of the party, having goods and canoes to carry from the Chicago River to the Des Plaines, lost sight of him, and he was never seen again. Autumn grass grew tall over the marshy portage, but they dared not set it afire, though his fate was doubtless hidden in that grass. The party divided and searched for him, calling and firing guns. Three days they searched, and daring to wait no longer, for it was November and the river ready to glaze with ice, they left him to some French people at the post of Chicago. But the child was not found. He disappeared and no one ever knew what became of him.

Like this is Henri de Tonty's disappearance from history. The records show him working with Le Moyne D'Iberville and Le Moyne de Bienville to found New Orleans and Mobile, pushing the enterprises which La Salle had begun. He has been blamed with the misbehavior of a relative of his, Alphonse de Tonty, who got into disgrace at the post of Detroit. Little justice has been done to the memory of this man, who should not be forgotten in the west. So quietly did he slip out of life that his burial place is unknown. Some people believe that he came back to the Rock long after its buildings were dismantled and it had ceased to be Fort St. Louis of the Illinois. Others say he died in Mobile. But it is probable that both La Salle and Tonty left their bodies to the wilderness which their invincible spirits had conquered.

After the settlement of Kaskaskia a strong fortress was built sixteen miles above, on the same side of the Mississippi. The king of France spent a million crowns strengthening this place, which was called Fort Chartres. Its massive walls, inclosing four acres, and its buildings and arched gateway were like some medieval stronghold strangely transplanted from the Old World. White uniformed troops paraded. A village sprang up around it. Fort Chartres was the center of government until Kaskaskia became the first capital of the Illinois territory. Applications for land had to be made at this post. Indians on the Mississippi, for it was a little distance from the shore, heard drumbeat and sunset gun, and were proud of going in and out of its mighty gateway under the white flag of France.

Other villages began on the eastern bank of the river — Cahokia, opposite the present city of St. Louis, and Prairie du Rocher, nearer Kaskaskia. Ste. Genevieve also was built in what is now the state of Missouri, on land which then was claimed by the Spaniards. There was a Post of Natchitoches on the Red River, as well as a Post of Washita on the Washita River. Settlements were also founded upon La Fourche and Fausse Rivière above New Orleans.

"The finest country we have seen," wrote one of the adventurers in those days, "is all from Chicago to the Tamaroas. It is nothing but prairie and clumps of wood as far as you can see. The Tamaroas are eight leagues from the Illinois." Chicago was a landing place and portage from the great lakes long before a stockade with a blockhouse was built called Fort Dearborn.

"Monjolly," wrote the same adventurer, "or Mount Jolliet, is a mound of earth on the prairie on the right side of the Illinois River as you go down, elevated about thirty feet. The Indians say at the time of the great deluge one of their ancestors escaped, and this little mountain is his canoe which he turned over there."

La Salle had learned from the Iroquois about the Ohio River. But the region through which it flowed to the Mississippi remained for a long while an unbroken wilderness. The English settlements on their strip of Atlantic coast, however, and the French settlements in the west, reached gradually out over this territory and met and grappled. Whichever power got and kept the mastery of the west would get the mastery of the continent.

The territory of Kentucky, like that of Michigan, was owned by no tribe of Indians. "It was the common hunting and fighting ground of Ohio tribes on the north and Cherokees and Chickasaws on the south."

There was indeed one exception to the uninhabited state of all that land stretching betwixt the Alleghanies and the Mississippi. Vincennes, now a town of Indiana, was, after Kaskaskia, the oldest place in the west. This isolated post is said to have been founded by French soldiers and emigrants. Five thousand acres were devoted to the common field. De Vincennes, for whom it was named, was a nephew of Louis Jolliet. And while it is not at all certain that he founded the post, he doubtless sojourned there in the Indiana country during his roving life. A small stockade on the site of the town of Fort Wayne is said to have been built by him.

French settlements began to extend southward from Lake Erie to the head waters of the Ohio, like a chain to check the English. Presqu'Isle, now Erie, Pennsylvania, was founded about the same time as Vincennes.

A French settler built his house in an inclosure of two or three acres. The unvarying model was one story high, with porches or galleries surrounding it. Wooden walls were filled and daubed with a solid mass of what was called cat-and-clay, a mixture of mortar and chopped straw or Spanish moss. The chimney

was of the same materials, shaped by four long
corner posts, wide apart below, and nearer
together at the top.

As fast as children grew up and married they
built their cottages in their father's yard; and
so it went on, until with children and grand-
children and great-grandchildren, a small village accumulated around one old couple.

The French were not anxious to obtain grants
of the rich wild land. Every settlement had
its common field, large or small, as was desired.
A portion of this field was given to each person
in the village for his own, and he was obliged
to cultivate it and raise food for his family. If
a man neglected his ground, it was taken from
him. A large tract of land called the common
pasture was also inclosed for everybody's cattle
to graze in.

Sometimes houses were set facing one court,
or center, like a camp, for defense. But generally the French had little trouble with their
savage neighbors, who took very kindly to
them. The story of western settlement is not
that dreadful story of continual wars with
Indians which reddens the pages of eastern
colonies. The French were gay people. They
loved to dance and hunt and spend their time

in amusements. While the serious, stubborn English were grubbing out the foundations of great states on the Atlantic coast, it must be confessed these happy folks cared little about developing the rich Mississippi valley.

During all its early occupation this hospitable land abounded with game. Though in November the buffaloes became so lean that only their tongues were eaten, swans, geese, and ducks were always plentiful, and the fish could not be exhausted.

On a day in February, people from Kaskaskia hurried over the road which then stretched a league to the Mississippi, for the town was on the Kaskaskia River bank. There were settlers in blanket capotes, shaped like friars' frocks, with hoods to draw over their heads. If it had been June instead of February, a blue or red kerchief would have covered the men's heads. The dress of an ordinary frontiersman in those days consisted of shirt, breech-cloth, and buckskin leggins, with moccasins, and neips, or strips of blanket wrapped around the feet for stockings. The voyageur so equipped could undertake any hardship. But in the settlements wooden shoes were worn instead of moccasins, and garments of texture lighter than buckskin.

The women wore short gowns, or long, full jackets, and petticoats; and their moccasins were like those of squaws, ornamented with beautiful quill-work. Their outer wraps were not unlike the men's; so a multitude of blanket capotes flocked toward the Mississippi bank, which at that time had not been washed away, and rose steeply above the water. They had all run to see a procession of boats pass by from Fort Chartres.

A little negro had brought the news that the boats were in sight. Black slaves were owned by some of the French; and Indian slaves, sold by their captors to the settlers, had long been members of these patriarchal households. Many of them had left their work to follow their masters to the river; the negroes pointing and shouting, the Indians standing motionless and silent.

The sun flecked a broad expanse of water, and down this shining track rushed a fleet of canoes; white uniforms leading, and brick-colored heads above dusky-fringed buckskins following close after. This little army waved their hands and fired guns to salute the crowd on shore. The crowd all jangled voices in excited talk, no man listening to what another said.

"See you—there are Monsieur Pierre D'Artaguette and the Chevalier De Vincennes and
excellent Father Senat in the first boat."

"The young St. Ange and Sieur Lalande
follow them."

"How many of our good Indians have thrown
themselves into this expedition! The Chickasaw nation may howl when they see this array!
They will be taught to leave the boats from New
Orleans alone!"

"But suppose Sieur De Bienville and his army
do not meet the Commandant D'Artaguette when
he reaches the Chickasaw country?"

"During his two years at Fort Chartres has
Sieur D'Artaguette made mistakes? The expedition will succeed."

"The saints keep that beautiful boy!—for
to look at him, though he is so hardy, Monsieur
Pierre D'Artaguette is as handsome as a woman.
I have heard the southern tribes sacrifice their
own children to the sun. This is a fair company
of Christians to venture against such devils."

The Chickasaws, occupying a tract of country now stretching across northern Mississippi
and western Tennessee, were friendly to the
English and willing to encroach on the French.
They interrupted river traffic and practiced

every cruelty on their prisoners. D'Artaguette knew as well as the early explorers that in dealing with savages it is a fatal policy to overlook or excuse their ill-behavior. They themselves believed in exact revenge, and despised a foe who did not strike back, their insolence becoming boundless if not curbed. So he had planned with Le Moyne de Bienville a concerted attack on these allies of the

Autograph of Bienville.

English. Bienville, bringing troops up river from New Orleans, was to meet him in the Chickasaw country on a day and spot carefully specified.

The brilliant pageant of canoes went on down the river, seeming to grow smaller, until it dwindled to nothingness in the distance.

But in the course of weeks only a few men came back, sent by the Chickasaws, to tell about the fate of their leaders. The troops from New Orleans did not keep the appointment, arriving too late and then retreating. D'Artaguette, urged by his Indians, made the attack with such force as he had, and his brave array was destroyed. He and the Chevalier

Vincennes, with Laland, Father Senat, and many others, a circle of noble human torches, perished at the stake. People lamented aloud in Kaskaskia and Cahokia streets, and the white flag of France slipped down to half-mast on Fort Chartres.

This victory made the Chickasaw Indians so bold that scarcely a French convoy on the river escaped them. There is a story that a young girl reached the gate of Fort Chartres, starving and in rags, from wandering through swamps and woods. She was the last of a family arrived from France, and sought her sister, an officer's wife, in the fort. The Chickasaws had killed every other relative; she, escaping alone, was ready to die of exposure when she saw the flag through the trees.

But another captain of Fort Chartres, no bolder than young Pierre D'Artaguette, but more fortunate, named Neyon de Villiers, twenty years afterwards led troops as far east as the present state of Pennsylvania, and helped his brother, Coulon de Villiers, continue the struggle betwixt French and English by defeating, at Fort Necessity, the English commanded by a young Virginia officer named George Washington.

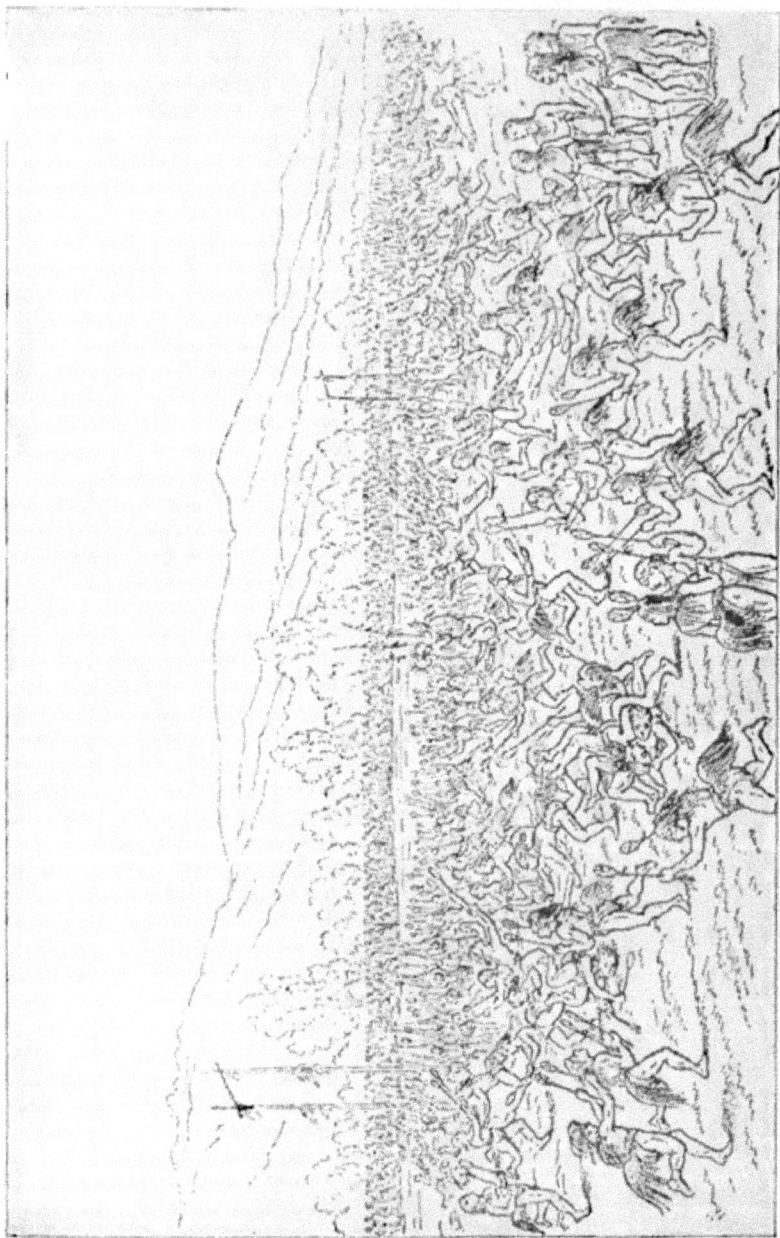

INDIAN GAME OF BALL.

After Catlin.

VI.

THE LAST GREAT INDIAN.

THE sound of the Indian drum was heard on Detroit River, and humid May night air carried it a league or more to the fort. All the Pottawatomies and Wyandots were gathered from their own villages on opposite shores to the Ottawas on the south bank, facing Isle Cochon. Their women and children squatted about huge fires to see the war dance. The river strait, so limpidly and transparently blue in daytime, that dipping a pailful of it was like dipping a pailful of the sky, scarcely glinted betwixt darkened woods.

In the center of an open space, which the camp-fires were built to illuminate, a painted post was driven into the ground, and the warriors formed a large ring around it. Their moccasined feet kept time to the booming of the drums. With a flourish of his hatchet around his head, a chief leaped into the ring and began to chase an imaginary foe, chanting his own deeds and those of his forefathers. He

was a muscular rather than a tall Indian, with
high, striking features. His dark skin was colored by war paint, and he had stripped himself
of everything but ornaments. Ottawa Indians
usually wore brilliant blankets, while Wyandots
of Sandusky and Detroit paraded in painted
shirts, their heads crowned with feathers, and
their leggins tinkling with little bells. The
Ojibwas, or Chippewas, of the north carried
quivers slung on their backs, holding their
arrows.

The dancer in the ring was the Ottawa chief,
Pontiac, a man at that time fifty years old, who
had brought eighteen savage nations under his
dominion, so that they obeyed his slightest word.
With majestic sweep of the limbs he whirled
through the pantomime of capturing and scalping an enemy, struck the painted post with his
tomahawk, and raised the awful war whoop.
His young braves stamped and yelled with him.
Another leaped into the ring, sung his deeds,
and struck the painted post, warrior after warrior following, until a wild maze of sinewy figures swam and shrieked around it. Blazing
pine knots stuck in the ground helped to show
this maddened whirl, the very opposite of the
peaceful, floating calumet dance. Boy papooses,

watching it, yelled also, their black eyes kindling with full desire to shed blood.

Perhaps no Indian there, except Pontiac, understood what was beginning with the war dance on that May night of the year 1763. He had been laying his plans all winter, and sending huge black and purple wampum belts of war, and hatchets dipped in red, to rouse every native tribe. All the Algonquin stock and the Senecas of the Iroquois were united with him. From the small oven-shaped hut on Isle Cochon, where he lived with his squaws and children, to Michilimackinac, from Michilimackinac to the lower Mississippi, and from the eastern end of Lake Erie down to the Ohio, the messengers of this self-made emperor had secretly carried and unfolded his plan, which was to rise and attack all the English forts on the same day, and then to destroy all the English settlers, sparing no white people but the French.

Two years before, an English army had come over to Canada and conquered it. That was a deathblow to French settlements in the middle west. They dared no longer resist English colonists pushing on them from the east. All that chain of forts stretching from Lake Erie down to the Ohio — Presqu' Isle, Le Bœuf, Venango,

Ligonier — had been given up to the English, as well as western posts — Detroit, Fort Miami,

The White Flag of France.

Ouatanon on the Wabash, and Michili-mackinac. The settlements on the Mississippi, however, still displayed t h e white flag of France. So large was the dominion in the New World which England now had the right to claim, that she was unable to grasp it all at once.

The Indians did not like the English, who treated them with contempt, would not offer them presents, and put them in danger of starvation by holding back the guns and ammunition, on which they had learned to depend, instead of their bows and arrows. For two years they had borne the rapid spread of English settlements on land which they still regarded as their own. These intruders were not like the French, who cared nothing about claiming land, and were always ready to hunt or dance with their red brethren.

All the tribes were, therefore, eager to rise against the English, whom they wanted to drive back into the sea. Pontiac himself knew this could not be done ; but he thought it possible, by striking the English forts all at once, to restore the French power and so get the French to help him in fighting back their common foe from spreading into the west.

Pontiac was the only Indian who ever seemed to realize all the dangers which threatened his race, or to have military skill for organizing against them. His work had been secret, and he had taken pains to appear very friendly to the garrison of Detroit, who were used to the noise of Indian yelling and dancing. This fort was the central point of his operations, and he intended to take it next morning by surprise.

Though La Motte Cadillac was the founder of a permanent settlement on the west shore of Detroit River, it is said that Greysolon du Lhut set up the first palisades there. About a hundred houses stood crowded together within the wooden wall of these tall log pickets, which were twenty-five feet high. The houses were roofed with bark or thatched with straw. The streets were mere paths, but a wide road went all around the town next to the palisades. Detroit was almost square in shape, with a bastion, or fortified projection, at each corner, and a block-house built over each gate. The river almost washed the front palisades, and two schooners usually anchored near to protect the fort and give it communication with other points. Be-sides the homes of settlers, it contained barracks for soldiers, a council-house, and a little church.

About a hundred and twenty English soldiers, besides fur traders and Canadian settlers, were in this inclosure, which was called the fort, to distinguish it from the village of French houses up and down the shore. Dwellers outside had their own gardens and orchards, also surrounded by pickets. These French people, who tried to live comfortably among the English, whom they liked no better than the Indians did, raised fine pears and apples and made wine of the wild grapes.

The river, emptying the water of the upper lakes into Lake Erie, was about half a mile wide. Sunlight next morning showed this blue strait sparkling from the palisades to the other shore, and trees and gardens moist with that dewy breath which seems to exhale from fresh-water seas. Indians swarmed early around the fort, pretending that the young men were

that day going to play a game of ball in the
fields, while Pontiac and sixty old chiefs came
to hold a council with the English. More
than a thousand of them lounged about, ready
for action. The braves were blanketed, each
carrying a gun with its barrel filed off short
enough to be concealed under his blanket.

About ten o'clock Pontiac and his chiefs
crossed the river in birch canoes and stalked
in Indian file, every man stepping in the tracks
of the man before him, to the fort gates. The
gates on the water side usually stood open until
evening, for the English, contemptuously careless of savages, let squaws and warriors come
and go at pleasure. They did not that morning
open until Pontiac entered. He found himself
and his chiefs walking betwixt files of armed
soldiers. The gates were shut behind him.

Pontiac was startled as if by a sting. He
saw that some one had betrayed his plan to the
officers. Even fur traders were standing under
arms. To this day it is not known who secretly
warned the fort of Pontiac's conspiracy; but
the most reliable tradition declares it to have
been a young squaw named Catherine, who
could not endure to see friends whom she loved
put to death.

It flashed through Pontiac's mind that he and his followers were now really prisoners. The captain of Detroit was afterwards blamed for not holding the chief when he had him. The tribes could not rush through the closed gates at Pontiac's signal, which was to be the lifting of a wampum belt upside down, with all its figures reversed. But the cunning savage put on a look of innocence and inquired : —

" My father," using the Indian term of respect, " why are so many of your young men standing in the street with their guns?"

" They have been ordered out for exercise and discipline," answered the officer.

A slight clash of arms and the rolling of drums were heard by the surprised tribes waiting in suspense around the palisades. They did not know whether they would ever see their leader appear again. But he came out, after going through the form of a council, mortified by his failure to seize the fort, and sulkily crossed the river to his lodge. All his plans to bring warriors inside the palisades were treated with contempt by the captain of Detroit. Pontiac wanted his braves to smoke the calumet with his English father.

" You may come in yourself," said the officer,

" but the crowd you have with you must remain outside."

" I want all my young men," urged Pontiac, " to enjoy the fragrance of the friendly calumet."

" I will have none of your rabble in the fort," said the officer.

Raging like a wild beast, Pontiac then led his people in assault. He threw off every pretense of friendliness, and from all directions the tribes closed around Detroit in a general attack. Though it had wooden walls, it was well defended. The Indians, after their first fierce onset, fighting in their own way, behind trees and sheltered by buildings outside the fort, were able to besiege the place indefinitely with comparatively small loss to themselves; while the garrison, shut in almost without warning, looked forward to scarcity of provisions.

All English people caught beyond the walls were instantly murdered. But the French settlers were allowed to go about their usual affairs unhurt. Queer traditions have come down from them of the pious burial they gave to English victims of the Indians. One old man stuck his hands out of his grave. The French covered them with earth. But next

time they passed that way they saw the stiff,
entreating hands, like pale fungi, again thrust
into view. At this the horrified French settlers
hurried to their priest, who said the neglected
burial service over the grave, and so put the
poor Englishman to rest, for his hands pro-
truded no more.

One of the absent schooners kept for the use
of the fort had gone down river with letters and
dispatches. Her crew knew nothing of the siege,
and she narrowly escaped capture. A convoy
of boats, bringing the usual spring supplies, was
taken, leaving Detroit to face famine. Yet it
refused to surrender, and, in spite of Pontiac's
rage and his continual investment of the place,
the red flag of England floated over that fortress all summer.

Other posts were not so fortunate in resisting
Pontiac's conspiracy. Fort Sandusky, at the
west end of Lake Erie; Fort Ouatanon, on the
Wabash, a little south of where Lafayette, in
the state of Indiana, now stands; Fort Miami,
Presqu' Isle, Le Bœuf, Venango, on the eastern
border, and Michilimackinac, on the straits, were
all taken by the Indians.

At Presqu' Isle the twenty-seven soldiers
went into the blockhouse of the fort and pre-

pared to hold it, lining and making it bullet-proof.

A blockhouse was built of logs, or very thick timber, and had no windows, and but one door in the lower story. The upper story projected several feet all around, and had loopholes in the overhanging floor, through which the men could shoot down. Loopholes were also fixed in the upper walls, wide within, but closing to narrow slits on the outside. A sentry box or lookout was sometimes put at the top of the roof. With the door barred by iron or great beams of wood, and food and ammunition stored in the lower room, men could ascend a ladder to the second story of a blockhouse and hold it against great odds, if the besiegers did not succeed in burning them out.

Presqu' Isle was at the edge of Lake Erie, and the soldiers brought in all the water they could store. But the attacking Indians made breastworks of logs, and shot burning arrows on the shingle roof. All the water barrels were emptied putting out fires. While some men defended the loopholes, others dug under the floor of the blockhouse and mined a way below ground to the well in the fort where Indians swarmed. Buildings in the inclosure

were set on fire, but the defenders of the blockhouse kept it from catching the flames by tear-
ing off shingles from the roof when they began
to burn. The mining party reached the well,
and buckets of water were drawn up and passed
through the tunnel to the blockhouse. Greatly
exhausted, the soldiers held out until next day,
when, having surrendered honorably, they were
all taken prisoners as they left the scorched and
battered log tower. For savages were such
capricious and cruel victors that they could
rarely be depended upon to keep faith. Pontiac himself was superior to his people in such
matters. If he had been at Presqu' Isle, the
garrison would not have been seized after
surrendering on honorable terms. However,
these soldiers were not instantly massacred, as
other prisoners had been in war betwixt French
and English, when savage allies could not be
restrained.

Next to Detroit the most important post was
Michilimackinac.

This was not the island in the straits bearing
that name, but a stockaded fort on the south
shore of Michigan, directly across the strait
from St. Ignace. To this day, searching along
a beach of deep, yielding sand, so different from

the rocky strands of the islands, you may find at the forest edge a cellar where the powder house stood, and fruit trees and gooseberry bushes from gardens planted there more than two hundred years ago.

Michilimackinac, succeeding St. Ignace, had grown in importance, and was now a stockaded fort, having French houses both within and outside it, like Detroit. After Father Marquette's old mission had been abandoned and the buildings burned, another small mission was begun at L'Arbre Croche, not far west of Fort Michilimackinac, such of his Ottawas as were not scattered being gathered here. The region around also was full of Chippewas or Ojibwas.

All these Indians hated the English. Some came to the fort and said to a young English trader named Alexander Henry, who arrived after the white flag was hauled down and the red one about to be hoisted : —

"Englishman, although you have conquered the French, you have not conquered us. We are not your slaves. These lakes, these woods and mountains were left to us by our ancestors. They are our inheritance, and we will part with them to none!"

Though these Ottawas and Chippewas were

independent of those about Detroit, they had eagerly taken hold of Pontiac's war belt. The missionary priest was able for a while to restrain the Ottawas. The Chippewas, gathered in from their winter's hunting, determined to strike the first blow.

On the fourth day of June, which was the English king's birthday, they came and invited the garrison to look at a game of ball, or baggattaway, which they were going to play on the long sandy beach, against some Sac Indians. The fortress gates stood open. The day was very warm and discipline was relaxed. Nobody noticed that squaws, flocking inside the fort, had tomahawks and scalping knives hidden under their blankets, though a few Englishmen afterward remembered that the squaws were strangely huddled in wrappings on a day hot for that climate.

The young English trader, Alexander Henry, has left a careful account of the massacre at Fort Michilimackinac. He did not go out to see the ball game, because he had important letters to write and send by a canoe just starting to Canada. Officers and men, believing the red tribes friendly, lounged about unarmed. Whitewashed French houses shone in the sun, and the surge of the straits sounded peacefully on the beach. Nobody could dream that when the shouting Indians drove the ball back from the farthest stake, their cries would suddenly change to war whoops.

At that horrid yell Henry sprang up and ran to a window of his house. He saw Chippewas filling the fort, and with weapons snatched from the squaws, cutting down and scalping Englishmen. He caught his own gun from its rack, expecting to hear the drum beat to arms. But the surprised garrison were unable even to sound an alarm.

Seeing that not a Frenchman was touched, Henry slipped into the house of his next neighbor, a Canadian named Langlade. The whole family were at the front windows, looking at the horrible sights in the fort; but an Indian slave, a Pani, or Pawnee woman, beckoned to him and hid him in the attic, locking the door and carrying away the key.

The attic probably had one or two of those tunnel-like dormer windows built in the curving roof of all French houses. Henry found a place where he could look out. He saw his countrymen slaughtered without being able to help them, and it was like a frightful night-

mare from which there was to be no awaken-
ing. Presently the cry rose:—

"All is finished!"

Then the Indians crowded into Langlade's
house and inquired whether any Englishmen
were hid there. So thin was the attic floor of
planks laid across joists, that Henry could hear
every word.

"I cannot say," answered the Frenchman.
"You may examine for yourselves."

Henry looked around the attic for some place
to hide in. Moccasined feet were already coming upstairs. Savage hands shook the attic door,
and impatient guttural voices demanded the
key. While some one went for the key, Henry
crept into a kind of tunnel made by a heap of
birch-bark vessels, used in the maple-sugar season. The door was opening before he could
draw himself quite out of sight, and though the
pile was in a dark corner, he dreaded displacing
some of the birch troughs and making a noise.

The Indians trod so close to him he thought
they must hear him breathe. Their bodies were
smeared with blood, which could be seen through
the dusk; and while searching they told Monsieur Langlade how many Englishmen they had
killed and the number of scalps they had taken.

Not finding any one, they went away and the door was again locked. Henry crept out of hiding. There was a feather bed on the floor and he stretched himself on it, so worn out by what he had seen and endured that he fell asleep.

He was roused by the door opening again. Madame Langlade came in, and she was surprised and frightened at finding him. It was nearly night and a fierce summer rain beat upon the roof, dripping through cracks of the heat-dried bark. Madame Langlade had come to stop a leak. She told Henry that all the English except himself were killed, but she hoped he would escape. She brought him some water to drink.

As darkness came on, he lay thinking of his desperate state. He was four hundred miles from Detroit, which he did not then know was besieged, and with all his stores captured or destroyed by the Indians, he had no provisions. He could not stay where he was, and if he ventured out, the first red man who met him would kill him.

By morning the Indians came to the house inquiring for Henry, whom they had missed. Madame Langlade was in such fear that they might kill her children if they found Henry

sheltered in the house, that she told her hus-
band where he was and begged to have him
given up. This the Frenchman at first refused
to do; but he finally led the Indians again to
the attic.

Henry stood up, expecting to die.

The Indians were all partially drunk and
had satisfied themselves with slaughter. One
of them seized Henry by the collar and lifted a
knife to plunge into his breast. White man
and red man looked intently at each other, and
the savage. perhaps moved by the fearless de-
spair in the young Englishman's eyes, concluded
to take him prisoner. Henry began to think he
could not be killed.

He found that the captain and lieutenant of
Michilimackinac were also alive and prisoners
like himself. The missionary priest was doing
all he could to restrain his maddened flock. At
a council held between Chippewas and Ottawas, Henry was bought with presents by a Chip-
pewa chief named Wawatam. who loved him,
and who had been absent the day of the attack.
Wawatam put Henry in his canoe. carried him
across the strait to Michilimackinac Island. and
hid him in a cave. which is now called Skull
Rock by the islanders, because Henry found

ancient skulls and bones in the bottom of it. As the island was held sacred by the Indians, this was probably one of their old sepulchres. Its dome top is smothered in a tangle of evergreens and brush. There is a low, triangular entrance, and the hollow inside is shaped like an elbow. More than one island boy has since crept back to the dark bend where Henry lay hidden on the skulls, but only a drift of damp leaves can be found there now.

The whole story of Alexander Henry's adventures, before he escaped and returned safely to Canada, is a wonderful chapter in western history.

The Indians were not guilty of all the cruelties practiced in this war. Bounties were offered for savage scalps. One renegade Englishman, named David Owen, came back from adoption and marriage into a tribe, bringing the scalps of his squaw wife and her friends.

Through the entire summer Pontiac was successful in everything except the taking of Detroit. He besieged it from May until October. With autumn his hopes began to dwindle. He had asked the French to help him, and refused to believe that their king had made a treaty at Paris, giving up to the English all

French claims in the New World east of the
Mississippi. His cause was lost. He could
band unstable warriors together for a common
good, but he
could not con-
trol politics in
Europe, nor de-
fend a people
given up by
their sover-
eign, against
the solidly ad-
vancing Eng-
lish race.

North America at Close of French Wars, 1763.

But he was
unwilling to own himself defeated while the
French flag waved over a foot of American
ground. This clever Indian, needing supplies
to carry on his war, used civilized methods to
get them on credit. He gave promissory notes
written on birch bark, signed with his own
totem, or tribe-mark — a picture of the otter.
These notes were faithfully paid.

When he saw his struggle becoming hopeless
eastward, he drew off to the Illinois settlements
to fight back the English from taking possession of Fort Chartres, the last French post.

They might come up the Mississippi from New Orleans, or they might come down the Ohio. The Iroquois had always called the Mississippi the Ohio, considering that river which rose near their own country the great river, and the northern branch merely a tributary.

Pontiac ordered the Illinois Indians to take up arms and stand by him.

"Hesitate not," he said, "or I will destroy you as fire does the prairie grass! These are the words of Pontiac."

They obeyed him. He sent more messengers down as far as New Orleans, keeping the tribes stirred against the English. He camped with his forces around Fort Chartres, cherishing it and urging the last French commandant, St. Ange de Bellerive, to take up arms with him, until that poor captain, tormented by the savage mob, and only holding the place until its English owners received it, was ready to march out with his few soldiers and abandon it.

It is told that while Pontiac was leading his forlorn hope, he made his conquerors ridiculous. Major Loftus with a detachment of troops came up the Mississippi to take possession according to treaty. Pontiac turned him back. Captain Pittman came up the river. Pontiac turned him

back.   Captain Morris started from Detroit, and
Pontiac squatted defiantly in his way. Lieutenant Frazer descended the Ohio.   Pontiac caught
him and shipped him to New Orleans by canoe.
Captain Croghan was also stopped near Detroit.
Both French and Spanish people roared with
laughter at the many failures of the coming
race to seize what had so easily been obtained
by treaty.

Two years and a half passed between Pontiac's attack on Detroit and the formal surrender of Fort Chartres.   The great war chief's
heart, with a gradual breaking, finally yielded
before the steadily advancing and all-conquering
people that were to dominate this continent.

The second day of winter, late in the afternoon, Pontiac went into the fort unattended by
any warrior, and without a word sat down near
St. Ange de Bellerive in the officers' quarters.
Both veteran soldier and old chief knew that
Major Farmar, with a large body of troops, was
almost in sight of Fort Chartres, coming from
New Orleans.   Perhaps before the low winter
sun was out of sight, cannon mounted on one
of the bastions would have to salute the new
commandant.   Sentinels on the mound of Fort
Chartres could see a frosty valley, reaching to

the Mississippi, glinting in the distance. That
alluvial stretch was, in the course of years, to
be eaten away by the river even to the bastions.
The fort itself, built at such expense, would
soon be abandoned by its conquerors, to sink,
piecemeal, a noble and massive ruin. The dome-
shaped powder house and stone quarters would
be put to ignoble uses, and forest trees, spreading the spice of walnut fragrance, or the dense
shadow of oaks, would grow through the very
room where St. Ange and Pontiac sat. Indians,
passing by, would camp in the old place, forgetting how the last hope of their race had
clung to it.

The Frenchman partly foresaw these changes,
and it was a bitter hour to him. He wanted to
have it over and to cross the Mississippi, to a
town recently founded northward on the west
shore, where many French settlers had collected,
called St. Louis. This was then considered
Spanish ground. But if the French king deserted his American colonies, why should not
his American colonists desert him?

"Father," spoke out Pontiac, with the usual
Indian term of respect, "I have always loved
the French. We have often smoked the calumet together, and we have fought battles

together against misguided Indians and the English dogs."

St. Ange de Bellerive looked at the dejected chief and thought of Le Moyne de Bienville, now an old man living in France, who was said to have wept and implored King Louis on his knees not to give up to the English that rich western domain which Marquette and Jolliet and La Salle and Tonty and many another Frenchman had suffered to gain, and to secure which he himself had given his best years.

"The chief must now bury the hatchet," he answered quietly.

"I have buried it," said Pontiac. "I shall lift it no more."

"The English are willing to make peace with him, if he recalls all his wampum belts of war."

Pontiac grinned. "The belts are more than one man can carry."

"Where does the chief intend to go when he leaves this post?"

Pontiac lifted his hand and pointed east, west, north, south. He would have no settled abode. It was a sign that he relinquished the inheritance of his fathers to an invader he hated. His race could not live under the civilization of the Anglo-Saxon. He would have struck out

to the remotest wilderness, had he foreseen to
what a burial place his continual clinging to
the French would bring him.   For Pontiac was
assassinated by an Illinois Indian, whom an English trader had bribed, and his body lies somewhere to-day under the pavements of St. Louis,
English-speaking men treading constantly over
him.   But if the dead chief's ears could hear,
he would catch also the sound of the beloved
French tongue lingering there.

A cannon thundered from one of the bastions.
St. Ange stood up, and Pontiac stood up with
him.

"The English are in sight," said St. Ange
de Bellerive.   "That salute is the signal for the
flag of France to be lowered on Fort Chartres."